Science For Kids:

39 Easy
Astronomy Experiments

Other Books in the Science for Kids Series

CHEMISTRY:

39 Easy Chemistry Experiments (No. 3596)

This first book in the series examines the makeup of substances and the changes that take place in them. It contains experiments for making hard water soft, testing for unknown substances, growing crystals, and more.

METEOROLOGY:

39 Easy Meteorology Experiments (No. 3595)

This book introduces readers to the study of our atmosphere and the forces that make our weather, providing experiments that demonstrate how the rotation of the Earth creates the trade winds, show how gravity and temperature create currents of air, show why a rainbow appears, show how to make a cloud, show how to make a wind gauge, and more.

Science For Kids:

39 Easy Astronomy Experiments

Robert W. Wood
Illustrations by Steve Hoeft

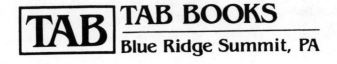
TAB BOOKS
Blue Ridge Summit, PA

FIRST EDITION
FIRST PRINTING

© 1991 by **TAB BOOKS**.
TAB BOOKS is a division of McGraw-Hill, Inc.

Library of Congress Cataloging-in-Publication Data

Wood, Robert W., 1933-
    Science for kids : 39 easy astronomy experiments / by Robert W.
Wood.
        p.   cm.
    Includes index.
    Summary: Experiments deal with such things as measuring celestial
bodies, making a spectroscope and telescope, photographing star
tracks, gravity, and growing plants in space.
    ISBN 0-8306-7597-3   ISBN 0-8306-3597-1 (pbk.)
    1. Astronomy—Experiments—Juvenile literature.   [1. Astronomy-
-Experiments.   2. Experiments.]   I. Title.
QB46.W88   1990
    522′.078—dc20   90-43544
                                                        CIP
                                                        AC

TAB BOOKS offers software for sale. For information and a catalog, please contact
TAB Software Department, Blue Ridge Summit, PA 17294-0850.

Questions regarding the content of this book should be addressed to:

Reader Inquiry Branch
TAB BOOKS
Blue Ridge Summit, PA 17294-0850

Acquisitions Editor: Kimberly Tabor
Book Editor: Judy Ramsey
Production: Katherine G. Brown
Cover photography: Susan Riley, Harrisonburg, VA

Contents

Introduction

The Science for Kids series consists of eight books introducing astronomy, chemistry, meteorology, geology, engineering, plant biology, animal biology, and geography.

Science is a subject that becomes instantly exciting with even the simplest of discoveries. On any day, and at any time, we can see these mysteries unfold around us.

The Science For Kids series was written to open the door, and to invite, the curious to enter—to explore, to think, and to wonder. To realize that anyone, absolutely anyone at all, can experiment and learn. To discover that the only thing you really need to study science is an inquiring mind. The rest of the material is all around you. It is there for anyone to see; you have only to look.

This book, *39 Easy Astronomy Experiments,* is the second in the Science For Kids series and explores one of the most exciting worlds of science—the field of astronomy. Astronomy is the study of the heavenly bodies and their movements. It is probably one of the oldest of the sciences. The earliest caveman gazed at the sky and wondered what he saw. As he looked up from his campfires, he noticed how the stars rose in the east and moved slowly across a giant dome in the night sky, then sank below the western horizon. As the wandering tribes gradually became farmers, they needed to know the proper times for planting and harvest. This led to the development of various types of calendars and required further celestial observations. These early calendars were based on the movement of the moon and other heavenly bodies. But they were often inaccurate. By the time of Julius Caesar, the lunar calendar had fallen three months behind. New calendars were made based on the movements of the sun during the year. These solar calendars were more accurate and today even our clocks are regulated by precise measurements of the movements of heavenly bodies.

Hundreds of years ago it was believed that the earth was at the center of the universe and the sun, moon, and stars moved around it once every day. Today we know that the earth is a planet that moves around the sun. The sun is a star and our star system, or galaxy, has about 100,000 million stars.

The largest telescopes show thousands of millions of these galaxies with each containing thousands of millions of stars, and almost all of them are moving away from us. The universe is expanding. We do not know how the universe began. One theory suggests that all of the material in the universe was created in one instant three to six billion years ago.

Our sun appears much larger and hotter than other stars only because it is closer. It is about 93 million miles away from the earth. This is a long way in miles, but not far at all astronomically. Because of the vastness of space, the mile is too short to be convenient. Instead, astronomers use the distance light travels in one year, a little less than six million, million miles. The nearest bright star, except for the sun, is Alpha Centauri. It is about 4.31 light years away. This is nearly 26 million, million miles from earth. This means that it takes the light from this star over four years to reach us. It also means that what we see in the universe is old news. If a star is 100 light years away, we would not see the light as it is now, but as it was 100 years ago. If you could sit on this star and look back at the earth with a powerful telescope, you might see life as it was in the 1890s. Railroads had finally crisscrossed the United States. The long cattle drives and the colorful era of the cowboy were coming to a close with the taming of the west. "Horseless carriages" chugged and snorted over unpaved roads. When we look at the stars, we are also looking back in time.

Life on other planets has long been a subject of speculation, but if there are so many millions of galaxies, and if each galaxy is made up of thousands of millions of stars, it seems to suggest that our sun would not be the only one that would have a planet that could support life. The mathematical odds would further suggest that life would be widespread in the universe. But the nearest intelligent form of life would be so distant that we could not contact them directly. Radio signals offer only a slight possibility of contact, and sending a space ship to a planet orbiting another star would take millions of years.

Our solar system is made up of the sun and the planets and other heavenly bodies that revolve around the sun. Our solar system is part of a giant galaxy called the Milky Way. Our sun is a little over half way from the center to the edge of the Milky Way, and revolves around the center of this mass of whirling stars at about 175 miles per second. Our earth and the rest of our solar system tag along with the sun at this dazzling speed. But it still takes over 200 millions years for our solar system to complete one revolution around the Milky Way. Our knowledge of the universe is constantly growing through advances made in astronomy. It is easy to see how astronomy will be an important field for the future exploration of space. Stargazing can be fun. Observing and studying the heavens can lead to a very interesting hobby. In fact many professional astronomers started by studying astronomy as a hobby.

To begin the study of this exciting science you need only good eyes and a dark night. Other studies might require binoculars or a telescope. A camera could be used for other experiments.

The experiments in this book are an easy introduction into the fascinating world of astronomy, but before you begin, be sure to read the *Symbols Used in This Book* section that follows. It warns you of all the safety precautions you should consider before you begin a project and whether or not you should have a teacher, parent, or other adult help you.

Completely read through a project before you begin to be sure you understand the experiment and you have all of the materials you'll need. Each experiment has a materials list and easy, step-by-step instructions with illustrations to help you.

Although you will want to pick a project that interests you, you might want to do the experiments in order. It isn't necessary, but some of the principles learned in the first few experiments will provide you with some basic understanding of meteorology and help you do later experiments.

Finally, remember that science should be fun. No experiment is ever a failure if you have learned something—even if you learn that something won't work as you predicted it. In fact, why not try applying some of your new knowledge about meteorology to deciphering your own local weather and how it affects those in your community. Part II explains how science fairs work and gives you some ideas on how to do a project such as the one I just mentioned.

Symbols Used in This Book

Carefully look over the symbols key below before beginning any experiment. These symbols mean that you should use extra safety precautions, or that some experiments require adult supervision. Before proceeding, *always* refer to this key whenever you see a warning symbol.

Science experiments can be fun and exciting, but safety should always be a first consideration. Parents and teachers are encouraged to participate with their children and students. Adult supervision is advised for very young children. Use common sense and make safety the first consideration, and you will have a safe, fun, educational, and rewarding experience.

 Materials or tools used in this experiment could be dangerous in young hands. Adult supervision is recommended. Children should be instructed on the care and handling of sharp tools.

 Exercise caution around any open flame or very hot surface such as a stove or hot plate. Adult supervision is recommended. Children should be instructed on how to handle hot materials and protect clothing, hair, and surfaces.

 Electricity is used in this experiment. Young children should be supervised and older children cautioned about the hazards of electricity.

PART I

Astronomy and Space

Experiment 1

Materials

- [ ] small lamp without the shade
- [ ] a globe or ball for the earth

The Sun and the Seasons

Use the lamp to represent the sun. If a ball is used for the earth, draw a circle around it to represent the latitude where you live. Then mark an X for your location (Fig. 1-1).

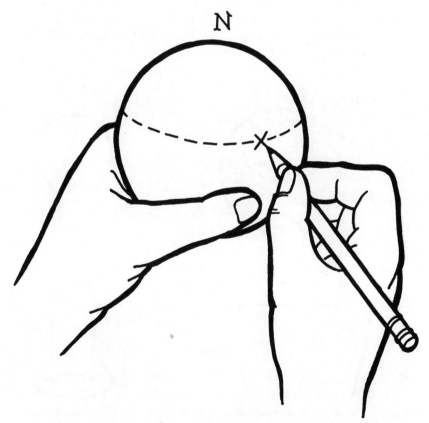

Fig. 1-1. *Mark your location on the globe.*

Hold the globe with its north and south axis straight up and down. Position it a few feet from, and on the same level with the lamp. Notice that half of the globe is lighted and the other half is in the shadow. Slowly spin the globe on its axis and observe your location. An easy way to remember which way to spin the globe is to rotate it counterclockwise looking down at the North Pole. Now move in a circle around the lamp, stopping at various positions, and rotate the globe. If the earth's axis were straight up and down, the lengths of the days and nights would not change (Fig. 1-2).

Now repeat the steps only this time tilt the globe about 23 degrees, as shown in Fig. 1-3. Keep its axis tilted the same as you move around the circle. Notice how the length of the days change. During half of the year, the North Pole is tilted toward the sun. In the Northern Hemisphere the days are longer than 12 hours. This is the spring and summer (Fig. 1-4).

During the other half of the year, the North Pole is tilted away from the sun. The days are now shorter and the nights longer. This creates the autumn and winter in the Northern Hemisphere. The seajust the opposite in the Southern Hemisphere. When one hemisphere is experiencing winter, the other is having its summer.

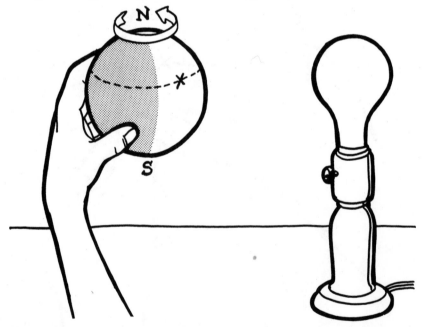

Fig. 1-2. *If the earth was straight up and down, the length of daylight would always be the same.*

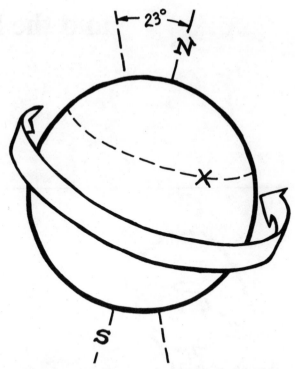

Fig. 1-3. *The earth's axis is tilted about 23 degrees from straight up and down.*

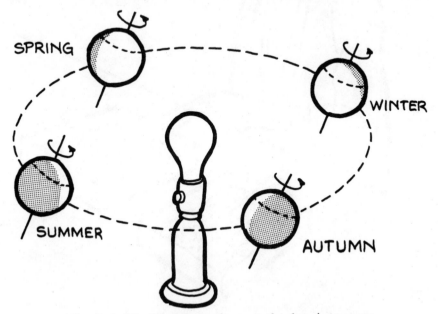

Fig. 1-4. *The tilt of the earth causes the changing seasons.*

Experiment 2

The Sun's Angle and the Seasons

Materials

- ☐ 2 small flat boxes
- ☐ 2 thermometers
- ☐ sand or dry dirt
- ☐ 2 small blocks
- ☐ sunlight

Fig. 2-1. *Place the end of the thermometers into the sand.*

Fill each box with an equal amount of sand or dirt. Place a thermometer in each box with its bulb buried about 1/4 inch (Fig. 2-1). Next place the boxes in the sun with one box supported by the two blocks. The blocks will keep the temperature of the ground from affecting the dirt in the box. The rays of the sun should strike this box at an angle. Place the other box so that the sun's rays strike it at right angles, directly at the box, not at an angle (Fig. 2-2).

Keep the boxes in the sun for about 15 minutes and compare the two temperatures. Notice that when the sun's rays strike the dirt at an angle, as in winter, the temperature is lower. This is because the rays, and sun's energy, are spread over a larger area and can't provide as much heat. In winter, the sun's rays also have to pass through more of the earth's atmosphere. When the sun's rays strike the dirt nearly straight down, as in summer, the energy is more concentrated and the temperature goes up. In summer, when the sun is directly overhead, the rays have fewer miles of atmosphere to pass through (Fig. 2-3).

Fig. 2-2. *The sun's rays strike one box directly and the other box at an angle.*

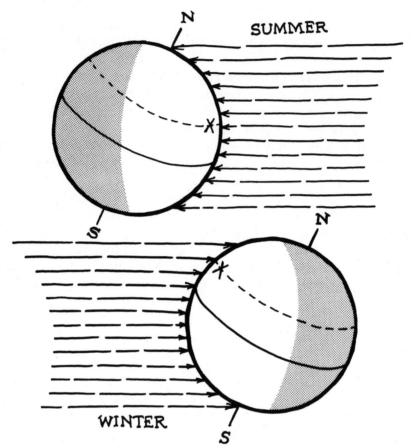

Fig. 2-3. *The summers in the northern hemisphere are warmer because the sun's rays strike the earth almost straight down.*

Experiment 3

Make an Eclipse

Materials

- ☐ 2 balls of different sizes
  (golf ball and soft ball)
- ☐ flashlight
- ☐ 1 or 2 books
- ☐ table
- ☐ dark room

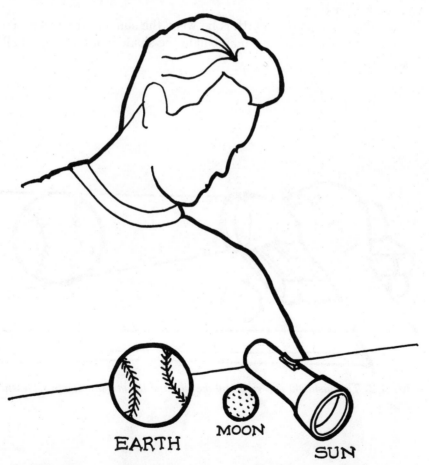

Fig. 3-1. To make an eclipse, all you need is a flashlight and two balls of different sizes.

A solar eclipse is when the sun is partially or totally hidden behind the moon. A lunar eclipse happens when the moon is partially or totally darkened by the earth's shadow. You can easily demonstrate an eclipse of either the sun or the moon (Fig. 3-1).

The large ball will represent the earth, the small ball will be the moon, and the flashlight will represent the sun (Fig. 3-2). Place the large ball, the earth, on the table and position the flashlight on the books so that it will shine level at the earth. Now hold the small ball, the moon, between the earth and the sun. Align the moon so that its shadow just touches the earth. Slowly move the moon to the side so that its shadow traces a path across the earth (Fig. 3-3). At a certain point along this path, the moon moves between the earth and the sun causing a solar eclipse.

In a lunar eclipse the earth is between the sun and the moon. To demonstrate this, place the small ball in the shadow of the larger ball (Fig. 3-4).

Fig. 3-2. *The flashlight will represent the sun and the larger ball can represent the earth.*

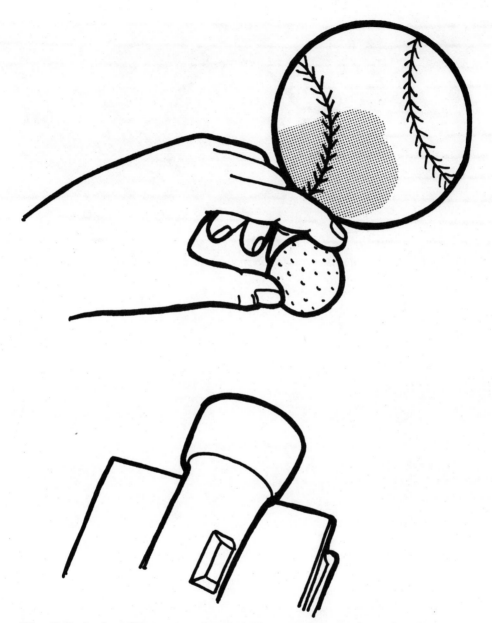

Fig. 3-3. *A solar eclipse occurs when the moon moves between the earth and the sun.*

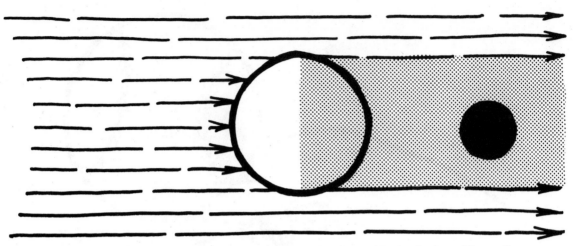

Fig. 3-4. *A lunar eclipse occurs when the moon is darkened by the shadow of the earth.*

Experiment 4

Angles in a Circle and a Clock

Materials

☐ a clock

The face of a clock can help you understand the number of degrees in a circle. A circle is divided into 360 equal parts, or degrees. These can be further divided into four quadrants, or quarter circles. Each quarter circle is made up of 90 degrees.

Look at the face of the clock and imagine one hand on 12 and the other hand on 3. This would represent 90 degrees (Fig. 4-1). With one hand on 12 and the other pointing to 6, 180 degrees will be shown (Fig. 4-2). When one hand points to 12 and the other one is on 9, 270 degrees will be displayed (Fig. 4-3). The full circle, or 360 degrees can be represented when both hands point to 12 (Fig. 4-4).

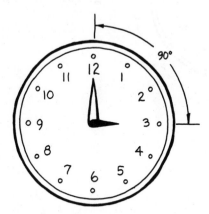

Fig. 4-1. One quadrant of a circle is divided into 90 equal parts called degrees.

Fig. 4-2. *One half of a circle has 180 degrees.*

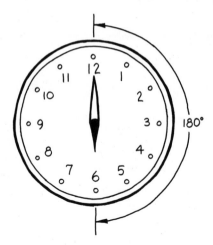

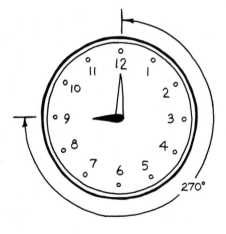

Fig. 4-3. *Three quadrants have 270 degrees.*

Fig. 4-4. *A full circle is divided into 360 degrees.*

Experiment 5

Time Zones and Lines of Longitude

Materials

☐ globe of the earth
☐ plastic clay
☐ 24 toothpicks
☐ 24 small paper squares

Examine the globe to find the lines of longitude. These are the lines that run from the North Pole to the South Pole. Find the 0-degree longitude line. It runs through a suburb of London, England, called Greenwich (Fig. 5-1). This is the prime meridian.

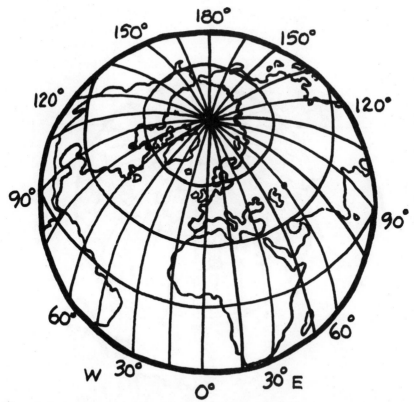

Fig. 5-1. *The 0 degree longitude line runs north and south through Greenwich, England.*

The sun moves over 15 degrees of the earth's surface each hour. For each 15 degrees west of Greenwich, the time is set back one hour. Find the line 15 degrees west of the prime meridian. Use the clay and attach a toothpick to this line. Mark a piece of paper with the number 1 and place it on the toothpick. Continue placing toothpicks every 15 degrees around the globe as shown in Fig. 5-2. Toothpick number 5 should be near New York. Number 12 should be on the 180 degree line. The time here is 12 hours behind Greenwich time. The 180th meridian is called the International Date Line. It is exactly halfway around the world from Greenwich. If you crossed the International Date Line from east to west on Sunday, the day would change to Monday. You lose a day. Traveling east, you gain a day. Imagine a new day beginning here. Continue attaching the toothpick starting over with number 1. Continue around the globe until you come back to Greenwich. Place number 12 there.

Looking at the numbers you can see that the new day begins on the western side of the date line (Fig. 5-3). As the earth rotates, this

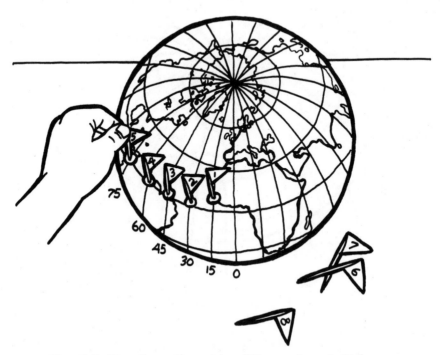

Fig. 5-2. *There is one hour of time difference for each 15 degrees.*

TIME ZONES

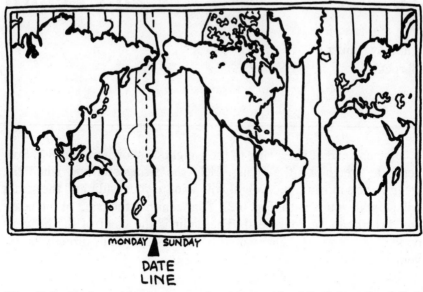

MONDAY SUNDAY

DATE
LINE

Fig. 5-3. *Each new day begins on the western side of the International Date Line.*

new day sweeps westward around the earth. This day will cover the entire earth in 24 hours. If you lived in New Zealand, you could celebrate New Year's Day 22 hours ahead of the people in Hawaii.

Experiment 6

Finding Your Nadir and Zenith

Materials

☐ string
☐ weight (key, sinker or small rock)

Tie one end of the string to the weight as shown in Fig. 6-1. Suspend the weight by the string. Hold the string still and when the weight stops moving, the weight will point to your nadir and the string will point to your zenith (Fig. 6-2). Your zenith is the point of the heavens directly above your head. The nadir is the point of the heavens opposite your zenith. This would be the lowest point, directly below your feet.

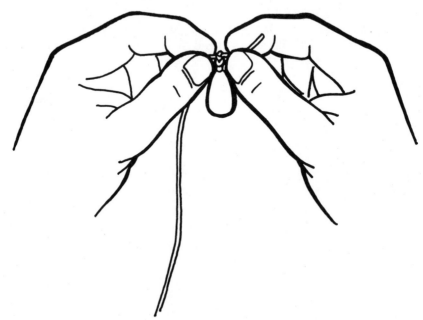

Fig. 6-1. *Tie a weight on the end of a string.*

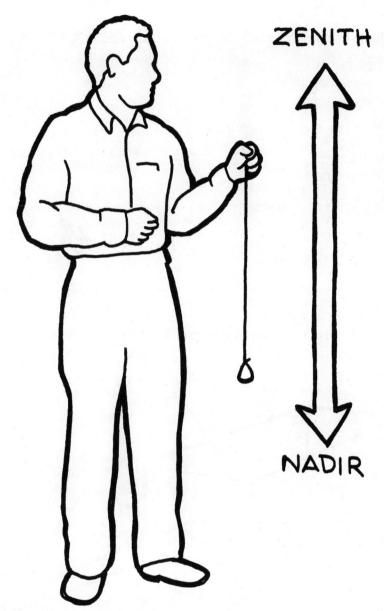

Fig. 6-2. *Suspend the weight and the string will point to your zenith while the weight points to your nadir.*

Experiment 7

How to Make a Spectroscope

Materials

- ☐ diffraction grating (inexpensive, purchased from scientific supply houses)
- ☐ small box with a lid (shoe box)
- ☐ 2 single-edged razor blades
- ☐ scotch tape
- ☐ hobby knife

Cut a small, round hole, smaller than the grating, in one end of the box (Fig. 7-1). Tape the grating over the hole as shown in Fig. 7-2. Make sure the lines of the grating run vertically (straight up and

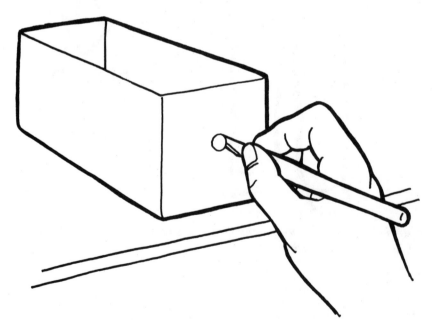

Fig. 7-1. *Cut a small hole in one end of the box.*

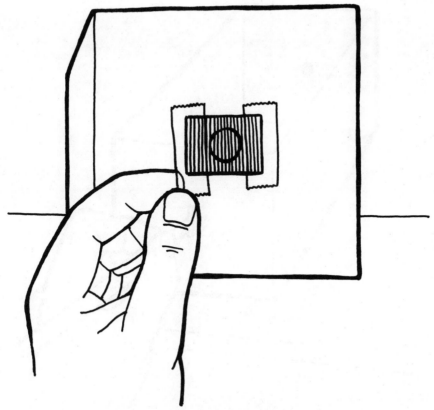

Fig. 7-2. *Place the grating over the hole.*

down). The grating can be protected by taping a thin piece of glass or plastic over it.

Directly opposite the hole, on the other end of the box, carefully cut a long, narrow slit. Make the slit vertical and about 1/4 inch wide and not longer than the width of the razor blade (Fig. 7-3). Next, tape the two razor blades over the narrow slit (Fig. 7-4). Place the blades so that the cutting edges face each other to form a narrow slit, with sharp edges, about 1 millimeter wide. This is about the width of a heavy pencil mark.

Now put the lid in place and tape the edges to keep out the light (Fig. 7-5).

Point the end of the box with the slit towards different light sources and look through the grating (Fig. 7-6). You will see a fringe of color on each side of the slit. Never aim your spectroscope at the sun

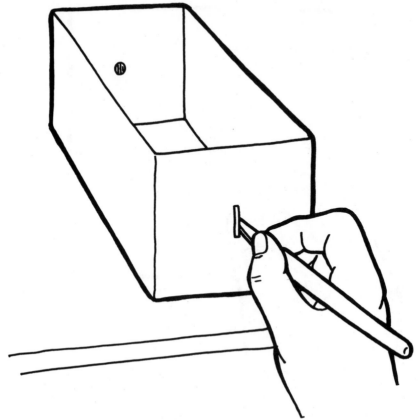

Fig. 7-3. *Cut a narrow slit in the other end of the box.*

but you can look at lights such as candles, light bulbs and fluorescent lamps.

The spectroscope is an important tool in astronomy. It separates the various colors, or spectrum, that make up light. The spectroscope is used with telescopes to determine the makeup of objects in the universe. Stars are classified according to their stellar spectrum. The main reason stars have different spectra is because of the difference in their surface temperatures. Any element that is hot enough, gives off certain colors of light. The spectrum of the light from each element is different from that of other elements. Astronomers use the spectroscope to separate the colors of a star, for example, to determine what elements are present.

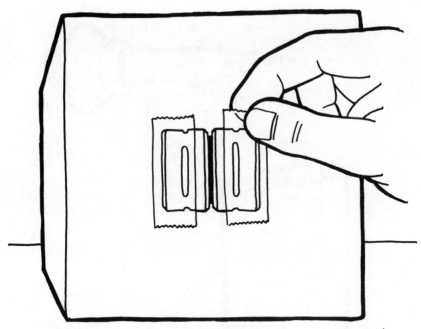

Fig. 7-4. *Tape the razor blades over the slit to form a narrow opening.*

Fig. 7-5. *Tape the lid to keep out light.*

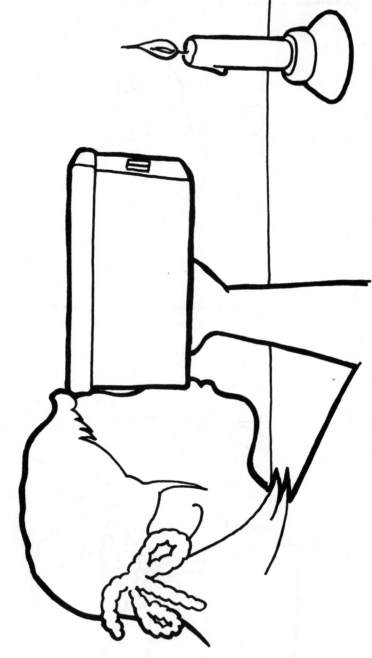

Fig. 7-6. The spectroscope separates the various colors that make up light.

Experiment 8

How to Measure the Diameter of the Moon

Fig. 8-1. *Cut a square in the center of a card.*

Cut a square in the middle of the card. Make each side of the square exactly 1/2 inch long (Fig. 8-1). Tape the card to the end of the support and fold it so that it stands upright, like a gunsight (Fig. 8-2).

Now aim the support at the moon. Sight along the support and move your head away from the card until the diameter of the moon just fills the 1/2-inch square (Fig. 8-3). Make a mark on the support even with your eye. Next, measure the distance from this mark to the card. You now have defined two triangles that will allow you to calculate the diameter of the moon (Fig. 8-4).

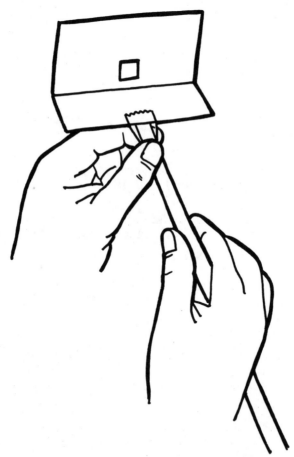

Fig. 8-2. *Attach the card like a gunsight.*

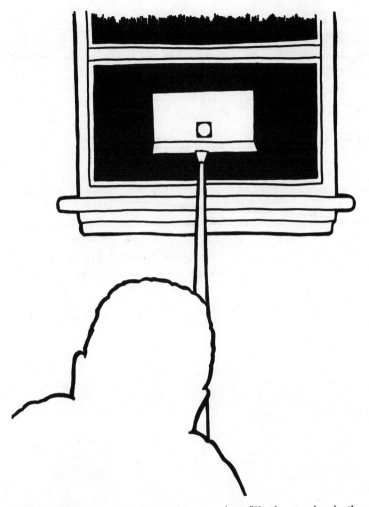

Fig. 8-3. *Position the card so that the moon just fills the opening in the card.*

The distance between the mark and the card should be about 55½ inches. The opening in the card is ½ inch. If you divide 55½ inches by ½ inch you get the number 111. The distance to the moon is about 240,000 miles. By dividing 240,000 miles by the ratio 111 from the first triangle you find the approximate diameter of the moon, 2162 miles.

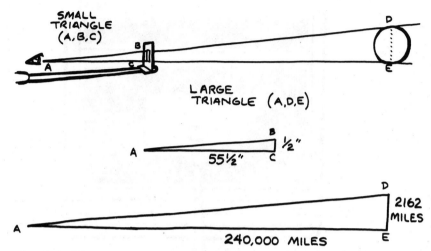

Fig. 8-4. Measure the distance from your eye to the card and you will have a triangle that will help you calculate the diameter of the moon.

How to Measure the Diameter of the Sun

- ☐ yardstick
- ☐ 2 white cards (3 × 5 inch index cards)
- ☐ scotch tape
- ☐ straight pin
- ☐ pencil
- ☐ know the distance to the sun (about 93 million miles)

This experiment is similar to experiment number 8. Remember, you should never look directly at the sun. However, you can use the sun's image that is produced on a card.

Make a small pinhole in the center of one of the cards (Fig. 9-1), fold it, and tape it upright to the 1-inch end of the yardstick (Fig. 9-2).

Fig. 9-1. Make a small pinhole in the card.

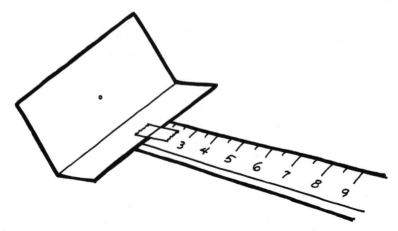

Fig. 9-2. *Tape the card to the yardstick.*

Make two small marks, 1/4 inch apart on the other card (Fig. 9-3). Hold this card upright about 2 feet from the card with the pinhole. Align the yardstick so that the sun's image appears on the card. The sun's rays pass through the pinhole to form the image and this makes two triangles. Adjust the card you're holding until the sun's image just fills the 1/4-inch space between the two marks (Fig. 9-4).

Fig. 9-3. *Make two marks, 1/4 inch apart on another card.*

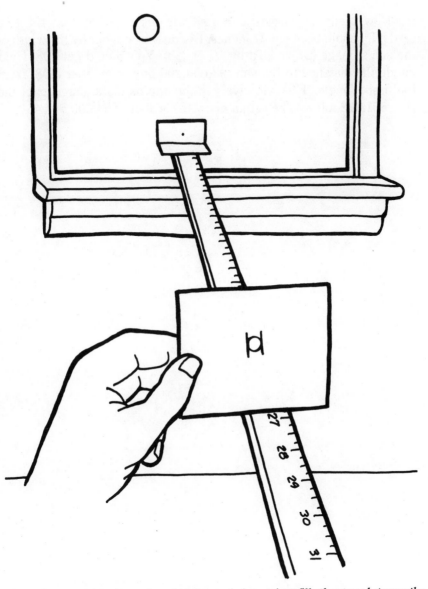

Fig. 9-4. *Position the card so that the sun's image just fills the space between the two marks. Measure the distance between the two cards for the triangle as in the previous experiment.*

Now read the yardstick to find the distance between the two cards. It should be about 27 inches. Divide this number by the width of the sun's image (27 divided by $1/4$ or .25). You should get 108. Next divide the distance to the sun, 93,000,000 by the number (108) from the first triangle. This will give you the approximate diameter of the sun, 861,112 miles. The actual diameter is about 864,000 miles.

Experiment 10

Materials

☐ ruler
☐ protractor
☐ pencil

Finding the Sun's Altitude

The altitude of the sun is its angle of elevation above the horizon (Fig. 10-1). If the sun is on the horizon, its altitude is 0 degrees. Halfway up would be 45 degrees and when it is directly overhead, its altitude is 90 degrees.

You can get a more accurate altitude measurement by holding a protractor and a ruler in one hand a pencil in the other. Place the straight edge of the ruler at the center of the protractor and stand the

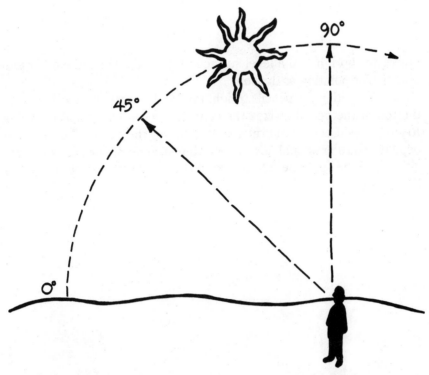

Fig. 10-1. The altitude of the sun is its angle above the horizon.

Fig. 10-2. *Stand the protractor upright on a level surface.*

protractor upright, on a level surface (Fig. 10-2). Have the other end of the ruler pointing at the sun.

Now position the pencil straight up and down where the shadow of the top of the pencil strikes the center of the protractor (Fig. 10-3). Rest the open end of the ruler on the top of the pencil. The straight edge of the ruler should now be pointing straight at the sun. Read the altitude of the sun where the edge of the ruler crosses the protractor (Fig. 10-4).

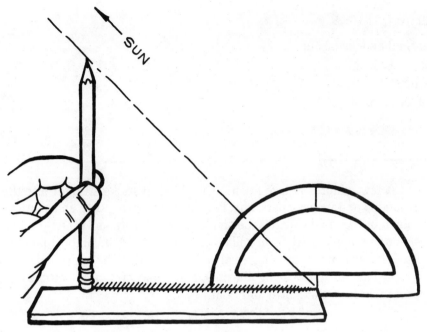

Fig. 10-3. *Stand the pencil so that its shadow falls to the center of the protractor.*

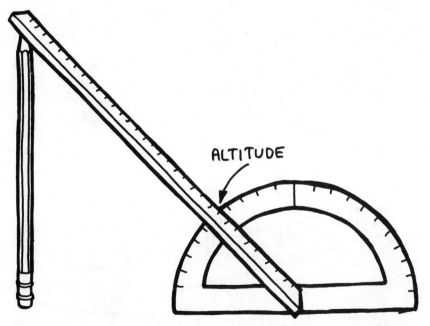

Fig. 10-4. *Read the altitude of the sun where the ruler crosses the protractor.*

Experiment 11

Finding the Meridian

Materials

- ☐ 2 straight sticks (about 12 inches long)
- ☐ hammer
- ☐ magnetic compass

A few minutes before noon, drive the two sticks straight into the ground, 3 or 4 inches apart, on a line approximately north and south as shown in Fig. 11-1. Watch the shadows of both sticks. When the two shadows are in line, the sun will be passing through its highest point in its daily sweep around the earth. This is called the meridian (Fig. 11-2). The sun is crossing the imaginary line of a great circle that passes through the North and South Poles.

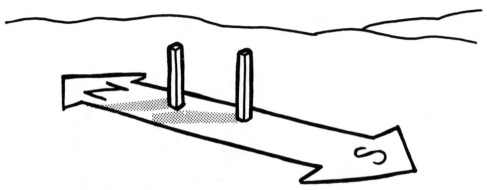

Fig. 11-1. *Drive two sticks into the ground a few inches apart.*

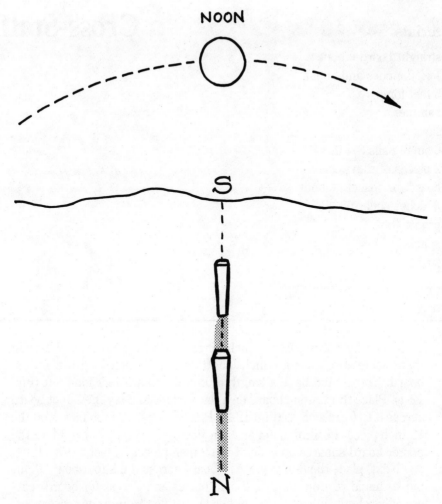

Fig. 11-2. When the shadows are in line, the sun will be at its highest point, the meridian.

Experiment 12

How to Make a Cross-Staff

Begin by cutting two, 2-inch lengths from the board and setting them aside. Next cut a 6-inch length and a 12-inch length from the board. You should have a length of board about 3 feet long left (Fig. 12-1). Place the 12-inch board on a flat surface and lay the 3-foot board across it to form a cross (Fig. 12-2). Place the two, 2-inch pieces on the 12-inch piece. Position them on each side of the 3-foot board. Place the poster board squares on each of the 2-inch pieces of wood (Fig. 12-3).

Next, place the 6-inch piece of board across the 3-foot board. This piece should rest on the two, 2-inch pieces and the poster board spacers. This should allow the 3-foot board to slide through the cross piece. When you have the pieces properly aligned, fasten them together using three nails on each side as shown in Fig. 12-4. Do not nail through the 3-foot board. It must be free to slide through opening you made using the other pieces.

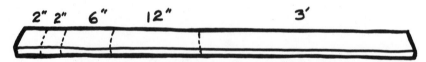

Fig. 12-1. *Cut the long board into the smaller pieces.*

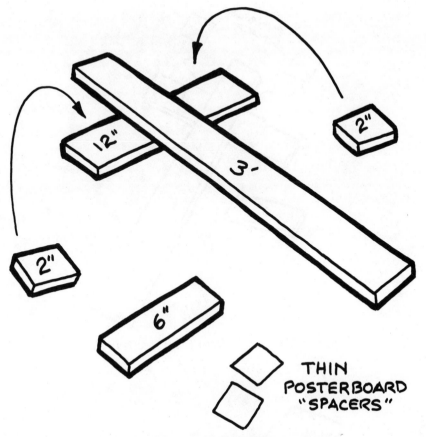

Fig. 12-2. *Assemble the pieces as shown.*

Now tie one end of the string to the end of the 3-foot board. Tie it so that the string can be pulled up over the edge of the board. Slide the cross piece down to the other end of the board. Stretch the string so that it will fall across the end of the cross piece. Next, place the protractor on the 3-foot board and, keeping tension on the string, read the angle of the string. Mark the angle of degrees on the 3-foot board (Fig. 12-5). You can mark the degrees in units of ten; 10, 20, 30, etc. Hold your cross-staff at eye level and aim the top of the long board at the horizon. Holding this level, move the cross piece until you can sight the North Star just above the tip of the cross piece. Read the number of degrees you marked on the long board. This should be your approximate latitude (Fig. 12-6).

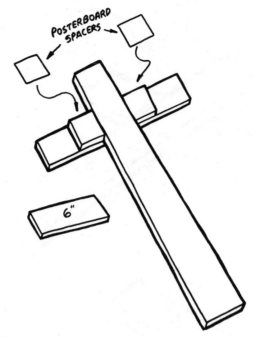

Fig. 12-3. *Put the poster board spacers in place.*

Fig. 12-4. *Fasten the pieces together with the nails.*

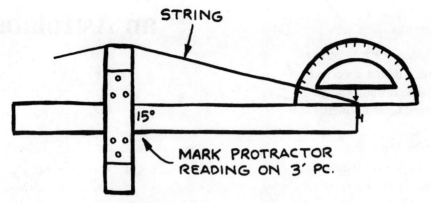

STRING

15°

MARK PROTRACTOR
READING ON 3′ PC.

Fig. 12-5. Mark the angle of degrees on the board.

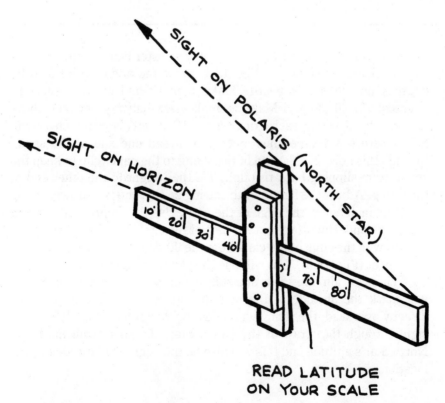

SIGHT ON POLARIS (NORTH STAR)

SIGHT ON HORIZON

10° 20° 30° 40° 70° 80°

READ LATITUDE
ON YOUR SCALE

Fig. 12-6. Sight on the North Star and read your degrees latitude on the board.

Experiment 13

How to Make an Astrolabe

Draw a line ½ inch from 2 sides of the poster board. With the protractor placed as shown in Fig. 13-1, draw the angles from 0 to 90 degrees on the poster board. Make a mark and number each 10 degrees; 10, 20, 30 etc. Make a small mark halfway between these numbers to represent each 5 degrees: 5, 15, 25 etc. Now punch a small hole where the degree lines meet and thread one end of the string through this hole. Tie the end of the string to the paper clip to keep the string from slipping back through. Tie the weight to the other end of the string. Adjust the length of the string so that the weight will swing about ½ inch below the edge of the card. Use the length of the string as a guide and trim off the excess part of the card (Fig. 13-2). Now tape the straw to the edge of the card from the 90-degree mark to where the lines meet (Fig. 13-3). You will use the straw to sight through.

When you aim the straw at a star (never look at the sun), the string will mark the altitude of the star in degrees. If you aim at a star directly overhead, the string will be on the 90 degree mark. When you sight through the straw at the North Star, the string will mark the North Star's altitude and this will also be the degree of latitude of your location.

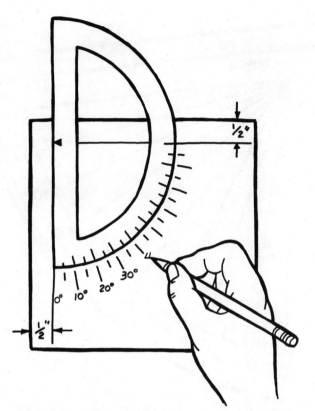

Fig. 13-1. *Mark off the degrees on the poster board.*

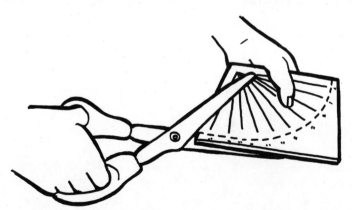

Fig. 13-2. *Trim off the excess part of the poster board.*

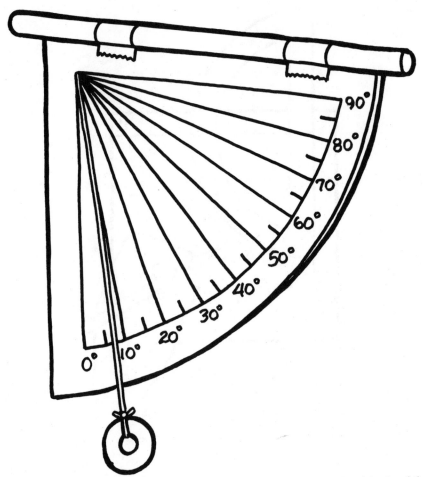

Fig. 13-3. *Sight through the straw and the string will show the altitude of the star.*

Experiment 14

How to Make a Theodolite

Cut a 1×2-inch piece from the cardboard and trim one end to a point to make the pointer. Glue it to one end of the 12 inch support as shown in Fig. 14-1. Make sure the pointed end is sticking out. You can use a crayon or marking pen to color it a bright color after the glue has dried.

Next, locate the center of the wood base and use the protractor to mark off a full circle. Mark the number of degrees on the base clockwise around the circle (Fig. 14-2). Next, use the large nail to make a hole through the center of the base. Work the nail around inside the hole so that the nail will turn freely. Remove the nail.

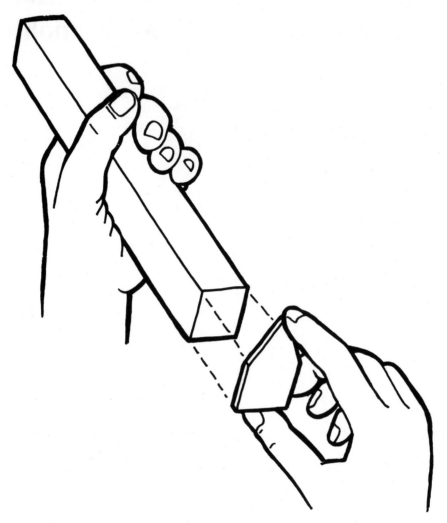

Fig. 14-1. *Glue the pointer to the end of the support.*

Now locate the center of the end of the support with the pointer. Use the large nail to make a guide hole. This hole can be only about 1/2 inch deep. Make sure the nail goes in straight. Turn the support upside down and place the flat washer over the guide hole. Slide the large nail through the base from the bottom up. Now place the point of the nail through the washer and into the guide hole. Drive the nail

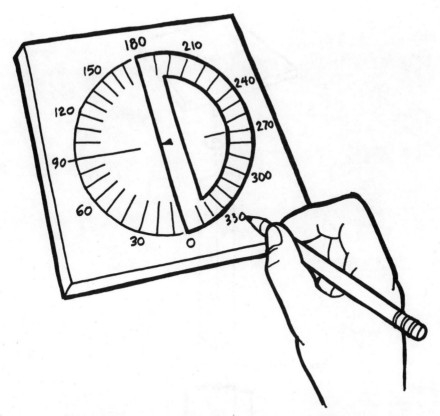

Fig. 14-2. *Mark off the degrees on the base.*

straight into the support (Fig. 14-3). Drive the nail far enough in so that the support fits snugly but the base is free to turn.

Tape the straw to the flat edge of the protractor. Align the pointer so that it points to 0 degrees when you sight through the straw. Use the small nail to mount the protractor to the support. The protractor must be free to turn. Next, tie one end of the string to the small nail and the other end to the weight (Fig. 14-4). When you place your theodolite on a level surface and sight the North Star through the straw, the pointer should point to 0 degrees. Do not move the base after you have it aligned north and south. Now when you sight a star, you can read its altitude on the protractor and its azimuth (angle along the horizon relative to north) on the base.

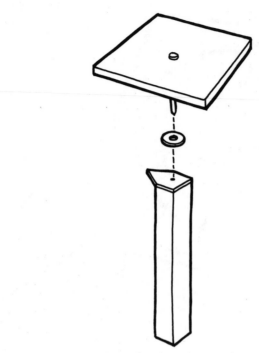

Fig. 14-3. *Attach the base to the support.*

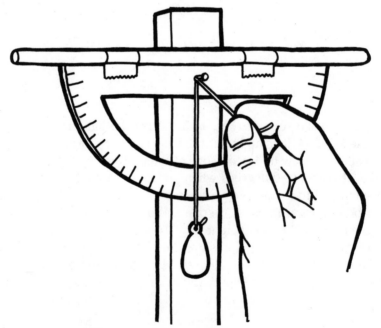

Fig. 14-4. *Suspend the weight from the small nail.*

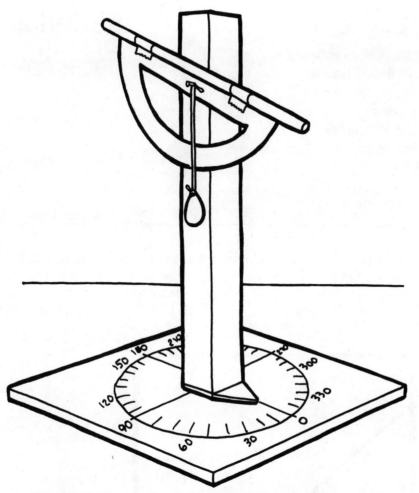

Fig. 14-5. *Now you can find the altitude of a star and its azimuth.*

Experiment 15

Materials

- [ ] a piece of thin cardboard
- [ ] wood or cardboard base
  (about 12 × 6 inches)
- [ ] protractor
- [ ] magnetic compass
- [ ] scotch tape
- [ ] pencil

How to Make a Sundial

The thin cardboard will be cut into a right angled triangle called a gnomon, but first you'll need to know the latitude of where you are. For example, if your latitude is 40 degrees this is the angle for the longest line of the triangle (Fig. 15-1). This is the sloping part. Draw the

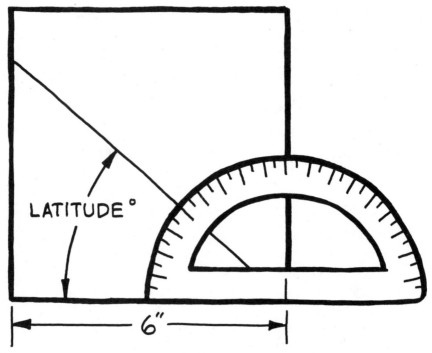

LATITUDE°

6"

Fig. 15-1. Mark your latitude on the card.

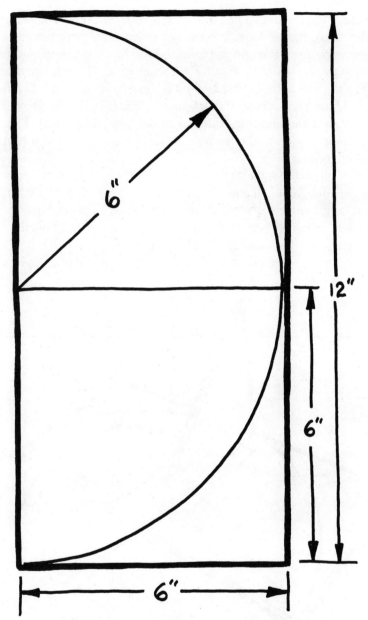

Fig. 15-2. *Draw a semicircle on the base.*

base line 5 inches long. Then draw the 90 degree corner. This line will be about five inches long. Now using the protractor, mark off a 40-degree angle from the end of the base line. Mark this line completing the triangle. It should be about 7³/₄ inches long. Cut out the triangle.

Mark a line across the 12 × 6-inch base dividing it into two 6-inch halves. Draw a semicircle with a 6-inch radius (Fig. 15-2). Use the tape to mount the gnomon (the triangle) to the base (Fig. 15-3). The sloping, 40-degree side of the triangle should be pointing to the center of the semicircle.

Now place the sundial outside and use the magnetic compass to align the triangle north and south. Position the sundial so that the 40-degree angle aims skyward toward the north. This means that the back side, or tallest part of the triangle, will be pointing north. To be more accurate, the sundial should be aligned true north instead of magnetic north. You could align it with the North Star at night.

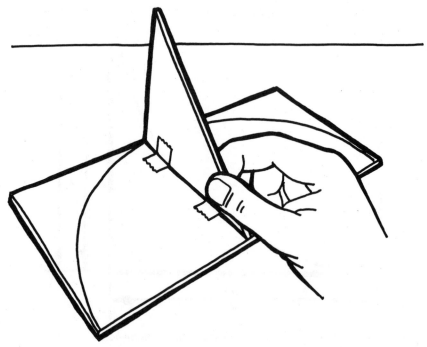

Fig. 15-3. *Attach the gnomon to the base.*

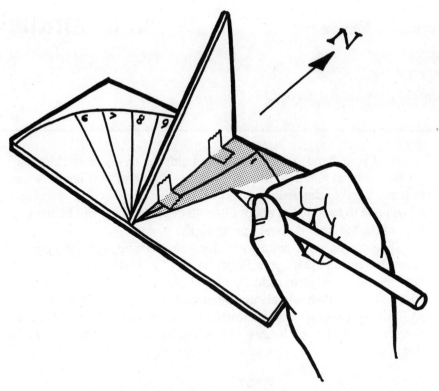

Fig. 15-4. *Mark the sun's shadow for each hour.*

After you have your sundial aligned, mark the position of the sun's shadow every hour on the base (Fig. 15-4). You should have numbers starting about six at the beginning of the semicircle going up to 12 noon at the back of the triangle, then going to about six in the afternoon. The 12 or so marks should be an equal distance around the half circle, and the number 12 should be pointing north. Your sundial will now tell you the time on a sunny day.

Experiment 16

Materials

☐ pencil
☐ sunny day

Using Your Hand as a Sundial

Hold your hand out flat with the palm facing up. Lay the pencil across the palm and hold the end with the thumb of that hand. As you grasp one end of the pencil with your thumb, the other end of the pencil will rise to an angle of about 30 or 40 degrees. This will be the gnomon of the sundial. It should point north.

When using your hand sundial in the morning, put the pencil in your left hand and point your fingers west (Fig. 16-1). In the afternoon, put the pencil in your right hand and point your fingers east (Fig. 16-2). The pencil should always point north. The shadow of the pencil will fall across your hand indicating the approximate time. Read the time from tip of your longest finger around the edge of your hand. Begin at six and count one hour for each fingertip.

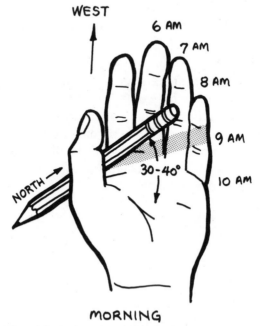

Fig. 16-1. Use your left hand in the morning.

54

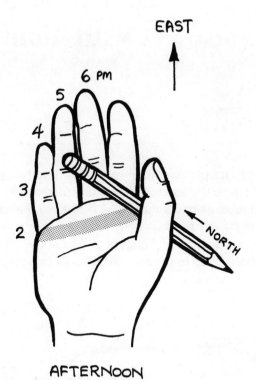

EAST

6 PM
5
4
3
2

NORTH

AFTERNOON

Fig. 16-2. *Use your right hand in the afternoon.*

Experiment 17

How to Measure Time with Your Fingers

Materials

☐ fingers
☐ sunny day

You can get an approximate measure of time by estimating how high the sun is above the horizon. Count one finger as 15 minutes (Fig. 17-1) or four fingers as one hour (Fig. 17-2). Face the sun and stretch your arms straight out in front of you. Stack your fingers one hand over the other and count eight fingers as two hours (Fig. 17-3). Measure from the horizon up to the sun. You should be able to tell approximately how long the sun has been up or how long until it sets.

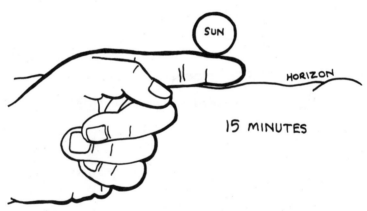

Fig. 17-1. *The width of one finger is equal to about 15 minutes.*

Fig. 17-2. *Count the width of four fingers as about one hour.*

2 HOURS

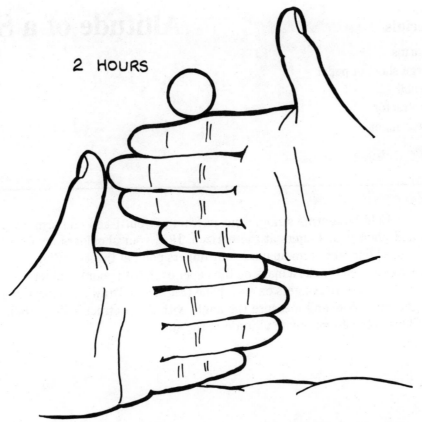

Fig. 17-3. *The width of the fingers on both hands will equal about two hours.*

Experiment 18

How to Estimate the Altitude of a Star

Materials

☐ 2 arms
☐ large sheet of paper
☐ pencil
☐ protractor
☐ clear night

Hold both arms straight out in front of you. Keep one arm level and point your fingers at the horizon. Hold your shoulders level and move your other arm up until your fingers point at the star (Fig. 18-1). Have a friend make a mark on the paper even with your shoulders and at the end of the fingers on each hand (Fig. 18-2). Draw a line between the three dots and measure the angle with the protractor (Fig. 18-3). This is the approximate altitude of the star.

Fig. 18-1. *Form an angle from the horizon to the star.*

Fig. 18-2. *Mark the corners on the paper.*

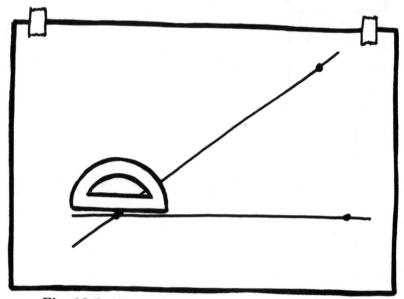

Fig. 18-3. *Measure the altitude of the star with a protractor.*

Experiment 19

Materials

☐ straight stick (about 12 inches long)
☐ sunny day

Finding North by the Sun

Drive the stick into the ground so that it points straight at the sun (Fig. 19-1). It should not have a shadow now. Wait about an hour. Now it will have a shadow (Fig. 19-2). The shadow might be about six inches long. It will be pointing east from the stick. The sun has moved farther to the west. This means that if you stand behind the stick with your right shoulder pointing east with the shadow, you will be facing north (Fig. 19-3). Your left shoulder will point west and your back will be facing south.

Fig. 19-1. *Drive a stick into the ground so that it points at the sun.*

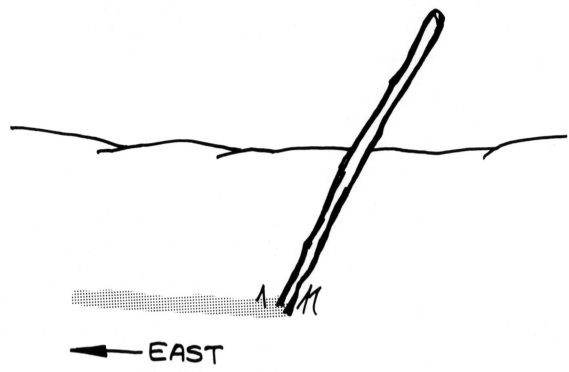

Fig. 19-2. *In about an hour the shadow will point east.*

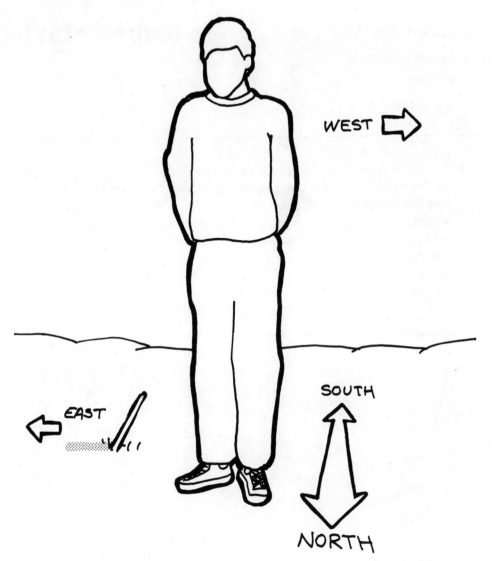

Fig. 19-3. *Point your right shoulder east and you will be facing north.*

Experiment 20

Finding Polaris (North Star)

Materials

- ☐ magnetic compass
- ☐ clear night

To find the North Star, face the northern half of the sky and look for the Big Dipper. It is made up of a group of seven bright stars that look like the side view of a pan with a handle, or a water dipper. In the winter, the handle of the dipper will be pointing down (Fig. 20-1), in spring, the dipper will be upside down (Fig. 20-2). In the summer, the handle will be pointing up (Fig. 20-3) and in the autumn, the dipper will be rightside up (Fig. 20-4). This is because it moves in a circle around the North Star.

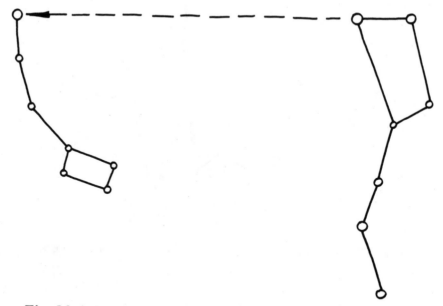

Fig. 20-1. *In winter, the handle of the Big Dipper will be pointing down.*

Now look at the two bright stars in the front of the dipper. They are the two stars farthest from the handle. They are called Merak and Dubhe, the pointer stars. They point to the North Star. Notice the distance between the two pointer stars. Measure about five of these spaces on a line from the end of the Big Dipper and you should find the North Star. It is also the end star in the handle of the Little Dipper.

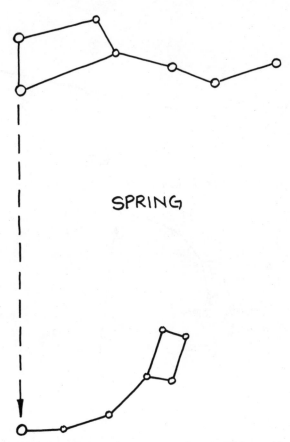

SPRING

Fig. 20-2. In the spring, the Big Dipper will be upside down.

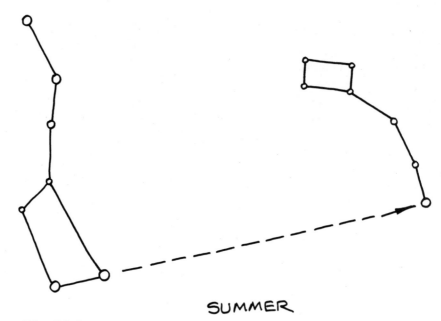

SUMMER

Fig. 20-3. *In the summer, the handle of the Big Dipper will be pointing up.*

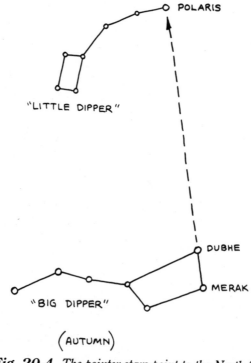

POLARIS

"LITTLE DIPPER"

DUBHE

MERAK

"BIG DIPPER"

(AUTUMN)

Fig. 20-4. *The pointer stars point to the North Star.*

Experiment 21

The Constellations that Turn around Polaris (North Star)

The red cellophane over the flashlight is to keep you from losing your night vision (Fig. 21-1). Take the star maps shown in Figs. 21-2, 21-3, 21-4, and 21-5 outside and look at the northern sky. Depending on your latitude and the time of the year, the view might be a little different from the one on the map. But the maps will show you what you should see from the northern hemisphere at about the middle of that particular season. Constellations that move around the North Star are called north circumpolar constellations.

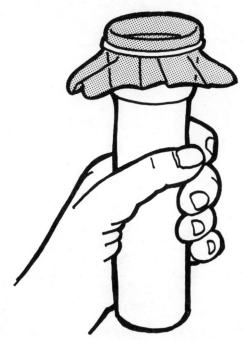

Fig. 21-1. *A red cellophane cover will help you keep your night vision.*

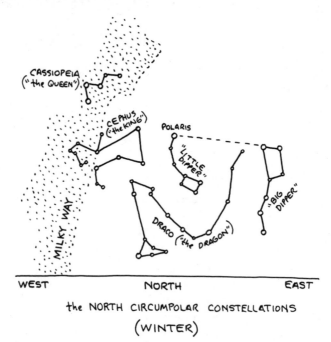

the NORTH CIRCUMPOLAR CONSTELLATIONS
(WINTER)

Fig. 21-2. *The northern sky in the winter will look something like the illustration, depending on your latitude.*

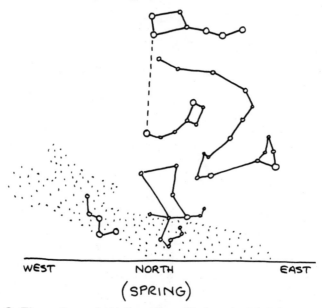

(SPRING)

Fig. 21-3. *The northern sky in the spring will show the Big Dipper upside down over the North Star.*

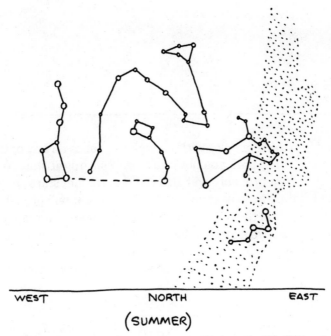

WEST   NORTH   EAST

(SUMMER)

Fig. 21-4. *The northern sky in the summer will show the Big Dipper to the west of the North Star.*

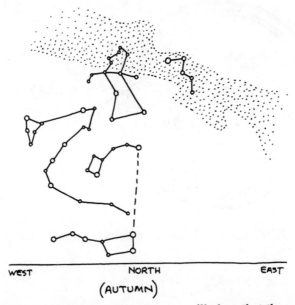

WEST   NORTH   EAST

(AUTUMN)

Fig. 21-5. *The northern sky in the autumn will show that the constellations have traveled, in a circle, about three-fourths the way around the North Star.*

Experiment 22   How to See Faint Stars

Materials

☐ clear night

Look into the night sky without trying to focus on any of the stars. Let your eyes drift until you notice a particular bright star. Now focus on that star. You probably will also see several dim stars surrounding the bright star. Now look at one of the dim stars. It will probably disappear. Look back at the bright star. The dim star should reappear. This happens because we all have a blind spot on the retina of our eyes (Fig. 22-1). This spot does not pick up very faint light. So when you want to see a very dim star, don't look directly at it. Look around it and it should appear.

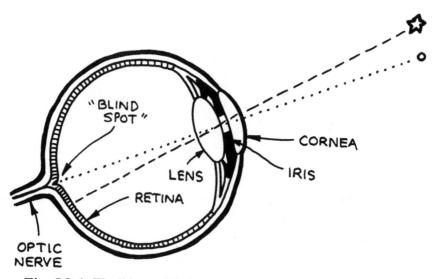

Fig. 22-1. *We all have a blind spot that keeps us from seeing faint light.*

Experiment 23

Tin Can Planetarium

Materials

- ☐ paper
- ☐ pencil
- ☐ tin can
- ☐ 2 or 3 different sized nails
- ☐ hammer
- ☐ flashlight
- ☐ dark room

Find an empty tin can that doesn't have any sharp edges. Wash the can thoroughly. Mark the area of the can on the paper as shown in Fig. 23-1. Then draw a constellation (Big Dipper for example) within the circle on the piece of paper. Mark the stars heavily so you can see them from the back of the paper (Fig. 23-2). Now turn the paper over

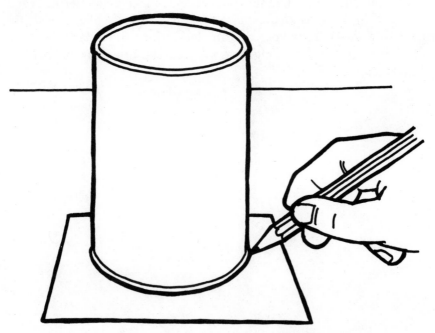

Fig. 23-1. *Mark the area of the can on the paper.*

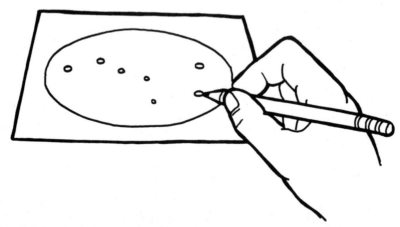

Fig. 23-2. *Mark the stars heavily so that they can be seen from the other side.*

and place it over the bottom of the can. Using different sized nails to show the different brightness of each star, make a hole for each star (Fig. 23-3). Now remove the paper and place the flashlight inside the can (Fig. 23-4). Take your tin can planetarium into a dark room and shine the light on the ceiling. You will see a star projection of your constellation.

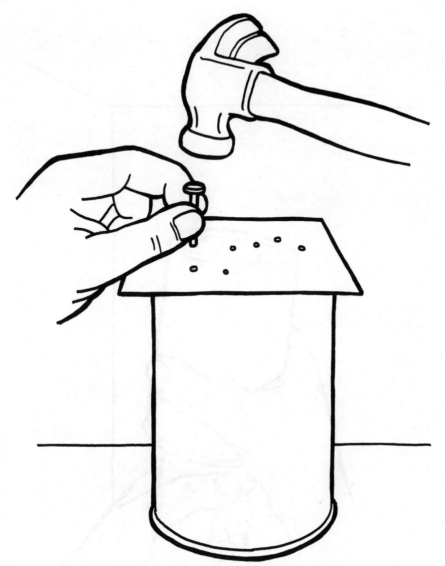

Fig. 23-3. *Turn the paper over and punch the holes for the stars.*

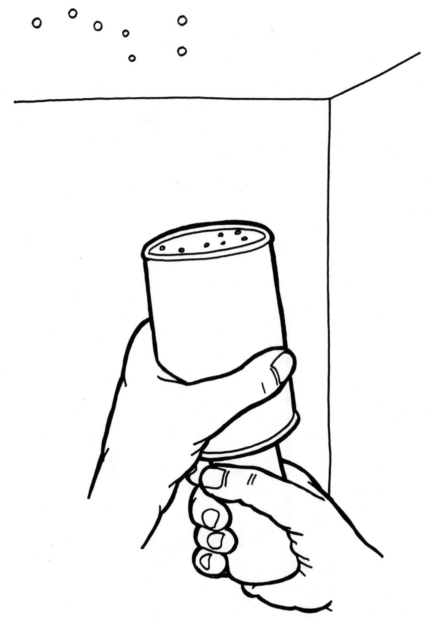

Fig. 23-4. *A flashlight shining in the can will project the constellation on the ceiling.*

Experiment 24

How to Find Venus

Materials

☐ clear morning or evening

The sun is the brightest object in our sky. The moon and then Venus are next brightest (Fig. 24-1). Venus is often called the morning or evening star. It is really not a star because it gives off no light of its own. The light we see from Venus, or any planet, is the light from the sun reflected from the planet's surface. Venus is bright because it is covered with clouds. These clouds reflect about 75 percent of the sun's rays. The earth has less cloud cover, so it reflects only about 40 percent of the sun's light.

Face the east just before sunrise, or the west just after sunset and find the brightest star. This will be Venus. It will always appear near the sun. Sometimes you might not see Venus because it is too close to the sun. Remember to never look directly at the sun.

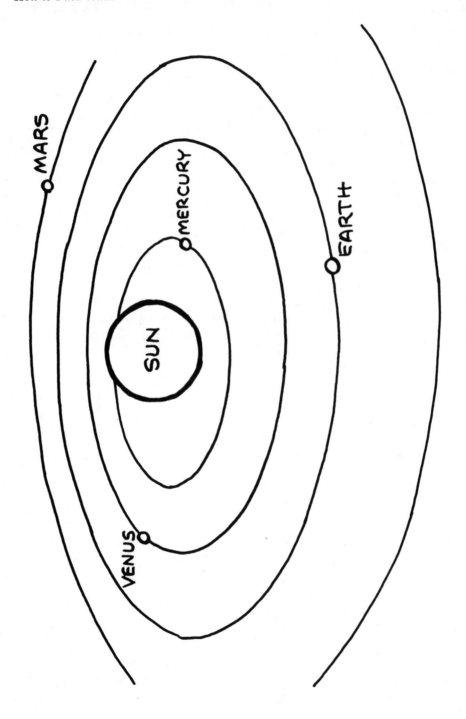

THE INNER SOLAR SYSTEM

Fig. 24-1. Except for the sun and the moon, Venus is the brightest object in our sky.

Experiment 25

How to Find Orion

Materials

☐ clear winter night
(February, between 9
and 10 o'clock)

Face south and look at a point in the sky about 45 degrees above the horizon. This is a point about halfway between the horizon and your zenith, or straight overhead. You will see a group of stars making up the constellation Orion (Fig. 25-1). It can be identified by four major stars with a line of three stars running at an angle near the center. The two brightest of the four stars are Betelgeuse and Rigel. Betelgeuse marks the right shoulder of Orion. Rigel is located at the left knee. Bellatrix is at the left shoulder and the three stars in line make up Orion's belt. Orion is named for the mighty hunter of Greek mythology. Figure 25-2 shows an artist's sketch of Orion.

Fig. 25-1. *Facing south on a clear winter night you can see the constellation Orion.*

ORION – the HUNTER

Fig. 25-2. *Orion was a mighty hunter in Greek mythology.*

Experiment 26

Why Stars Twinkle

Materials

- ☐ empty cereal box
- ☐ flashlight
- ☐ electric hot plate or stove
- ☐ small nail
- ☐ table
- ☐ dark room

Use the nail to punch a few small holes in one side of the cereal box (Fig. 26-1). Turn the flashlight on and put it inside the box (Fig. 26-2). Close the flaps on the box so that no light escapes except through the holes you made. The light from the holes represents the stars.

Place the box at one end of a table or counter with the holes facing the other end. Place the hot plate in the middle of the table and turn it on. Switch off the room lights and move to the other end of the table. Look at the lights from the box through the warm air rising from the hot plate. The tiny lights from the box will twinkle like stars (Fig. 26-3). The warm air rising from the hot plate moves up with varying temperatures. These different temperatures cause the air to have a variety of densities.

When the beam of light travels from the air of one density to another, it bends slightly. When a light beam bends, it is refracted. The earth's atmosphere moves in a similar manner with varying temperatures and densities. The movement of the layers of atmosphere bend and scatter starlight so that they seem to twinkle. In space, stars do not really twinkle.

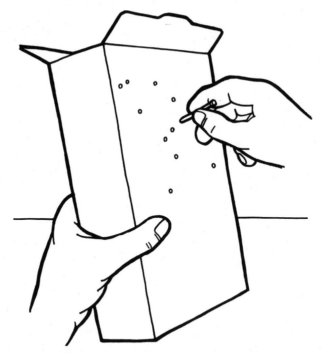

Fig. 26-1. *Punch a few small holes in the side of the box.*

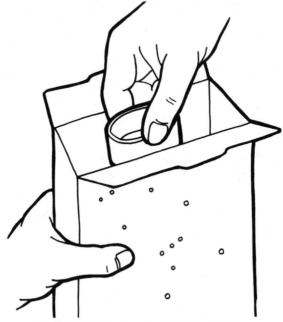

Fig. 26-2. *Put the flashlight inside the box.*

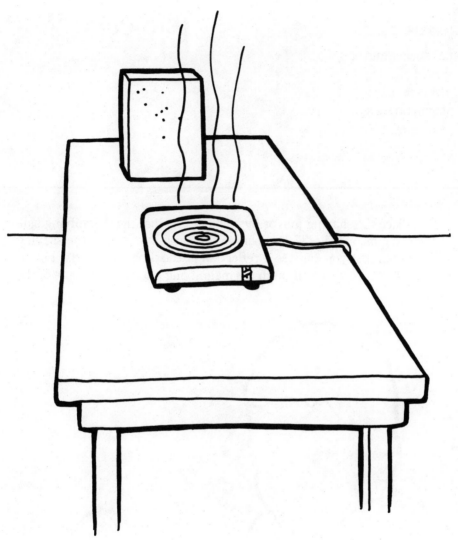

Fig. 26-3. *The warm air causes the lights to seem to twinkle.*

Experiment 27

How a Reflecting Telescope Works

Materials

- ☐ flat pocket mirror
- ☐ curved shaving or make-up mirror
- ☐ magnifying glass
- ☐ moonlight

Place the shaving mirror by a window so that the magnifying side faces the moon (Fig. 27-1). Position the flat mirror facing the shaving mirror so that you can see a reflection of the moon in the flat mirror (Fig. 27-2). Now look through the magnifying glass at the image of the

Fig. 27-1. *Place the magnifying side of the mirror towards the moon.*

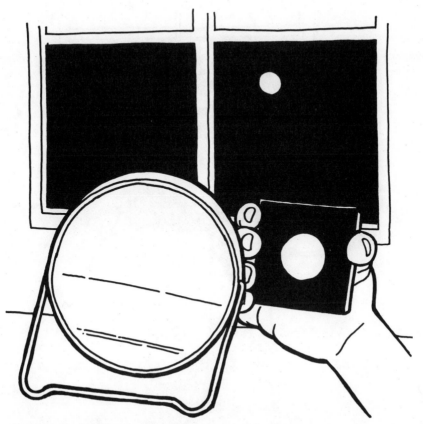

Fig. 27-2. *Position the flat mirror so you can see the reflection of the moon.*

moon in the flat mirror. It will appear much closer (Fig. 27-3), as if you were using a telescope.

Light traveling from the moon strikes the curved surface of the shaving mirror. Here it is reflected to the small, flat mirror where it is again reflected through the magnifying lens. The larger, curved mirror gathers light and concentrates it on the flat mirror. The magnifying lens magnifies the image of the moon.

Isaac Newton constructed the first reflecting telescope (Fig. 27-4).

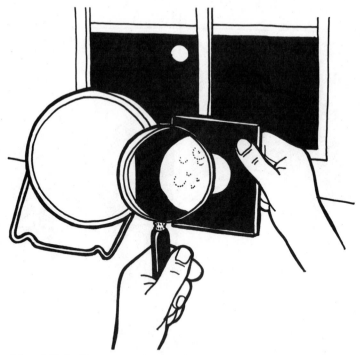

Fig. 27-3. *Use a magnifying glass to observe the reflected image of the moon.*

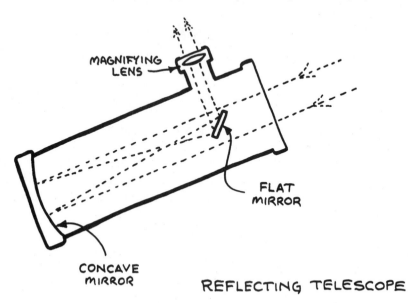

Fig. 27-4. *The curved mirror concentrates the image on the flat mirror, and the magnifying lens magnifies the image.*

Experiment 28

How to Build a Refracting Telescope

Materials

- ☐ small, thick convex lens (about 1/2 inch in diameter)
- ☐ large, thin convex lens (about 1 1/2 inch in diameter)
- ☐ cardboard tube (about 1 × 8 1/2 inches long)
- ☐ slightly larger cardboard tube (about 1 1/2 × 8 1/2 inches long)
- ☐ 2 small pieces of cardboard (to hold the small lens)
- ☐ glue
- ☐ strips of felt
- ☐ scissors or hobby knife

Lenses can be obtained from old cameras, magnifying glasses or other optical devices. The size of the cardboard tubes depends a lot on how large the lenses are. Mailing tubes or tubes from paper towels can be used. If these are not the right size, tubes can be rolled from cardboard or poster board.

Cut out two round cardboard disks to hold the small lens (Fig. 28-1). Cut holes in the disks slightly smaller than the diameter of the small lens (Fig. 28-2). Glue one of the disks just inside one end of the smaller tube (Fig. 28-3). Fit the small lens in the end of the tube. Now place the other disk next to the lens and in the end of the tube. It should be about flush with the end of the tube. Fasten it in place with glue (Fig. 28-4).

Fig. 28-1. *Cut out two disks to hold the small lens.*

Place the larger lens in one end of the larger tube. Position the tubes so that the lenses will be at opposite ends of the two tubes. The smaller tube will need to slide smoothly in and out of the larger tube. Glue strips of felt around the outside of the smaller tube to fill in the gap (Fig. 28-5). Add enough layers so that it fits close but is still able to slide easily.

Light from the object being viewed is gathered by the larger lens called the objective lens. It is then focused on the smaller lens. The smaller lens, called the eyepiece, further magnifies the image (Fig. 28-6).

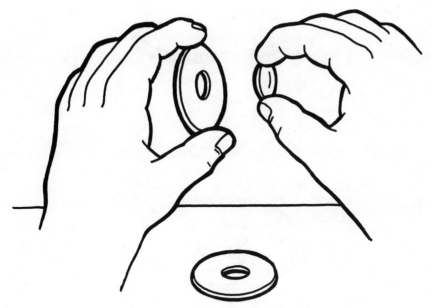

Fig. 28-2. *Cut holes in the disks to look through.*

Fig. 28-3. *Glue one of the disks inside the tube.*

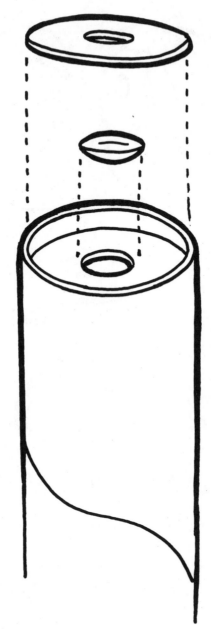

Fig. 28-4. *Put the lens over the hole and glue the other disk in place.*

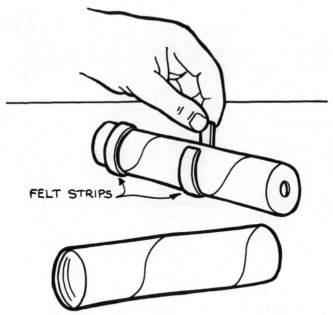

Fig. 28-5. *Felt strips will fill the space between the tubes.*

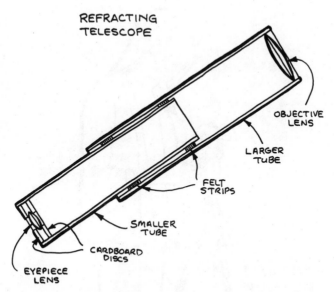

Fig. 28-6. *Light is gathered by the objective lens and focused on the eyepiece.*

Experiment 29

How to Photograph Star Tracks

Pick a clear night and try to find a location that is well away from other lights such as street lights or lights from houses. Load the film into the camera and mount the camera on the tripod (Fig. 29-1). Set the shutter speed so that the shutter will stay open for 30 minutes to one hour. You can aim the camera in any direction, but an interesting

Fig. 29-1. *Mount the camera on a tripod.*

pattern of star tracks can be photographed by aiming it at the North
Star (Fig. 29-2). Center the North Star in the view finder and take the
picture. Use a release cable if you have the shutter on the "manual"
setting (Fig. 29-3). It is very important to keep the camera steady during the exposure. Once your film is developed, you should see an interesting pattern of star tracks (Fig. 29-4).

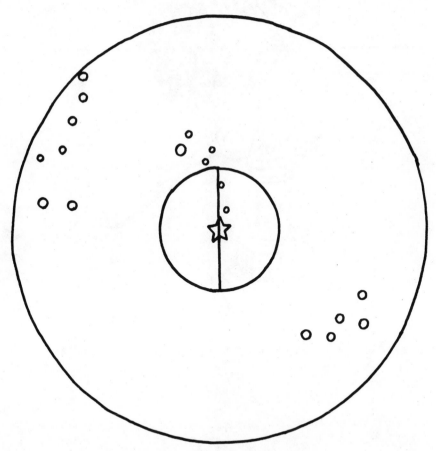

Fig. 29-2. *Focus the camera on the North Star.*

Fig. 29-3. *Use a release cable if you use a "manual" setting.*

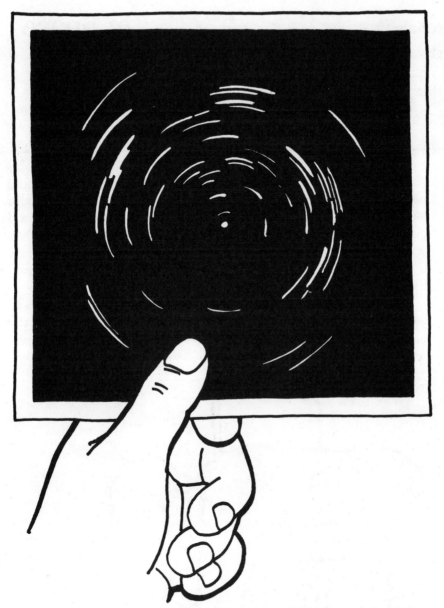

Fig. 29-4. *A time exposure will produce an interesting pattern of star tracks.*

Experiment 30

Eating and Drinking in Space

Materials

- [ ] glass of water
- [ ] drinking straw
- [ ] chair

Place the glass of water on the floor and lie across the chair. You'll need to be in a position where your stomach is higher than your mouth as shown in Fig. 30-1. Now bend your head down toward the glass and get a drink. You can use your hands. Just keep your mouth lower than your stomach. Notice how difficult it is to drink. Now use the straw (Fig. 30-2). It is still not easy. You have to overcome the force of gravity.

The weightlessness of space makes it necessary for astronauts to use things like plastic bottles and bags (Fig. 30-3). By squeezing the plastic bottle, or bag, with your hand, you provide the necessary pres-

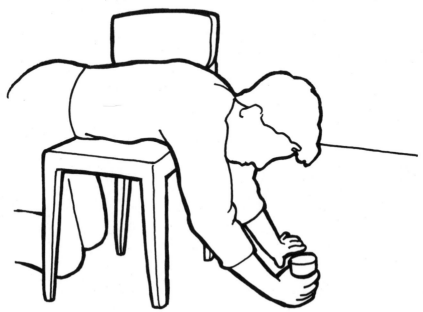

Fig. 30-1. Position your stomach higher than your mouth.

Fig. 30-2. *Try to drink through a straw.*

sure to move the food into your mouth. Once inside your mouth, the muscles in your throat move the food to your stomach. Without gravity, your body fluids do not drain as they would on earth. This might cause you to have the symptoms of a cold: runny nose, fluids in your chest and loss of senses of smell and taste. Also, if the air in the spacecraft were not circulated by fans, you would suffocate in your own breath. The carbon dioxide from your breath would stay around your face and you would soon choke.

Fig. 30-3. *Plastic bottles help astronauts eat and drink in space.*

Experiment 31

Materials

- ☐ swing, or bathroom scales and an elevator

How to Experience G-Forces

Get into a swing and start it moving. Notice at the bottom of the swing you feel heavier than at the top of the swing (Fig. 31-1). There, for a brief moment, you feel like you're floating. At the bottom of the swing, you feel your body being pulled down. This is caused by grav-

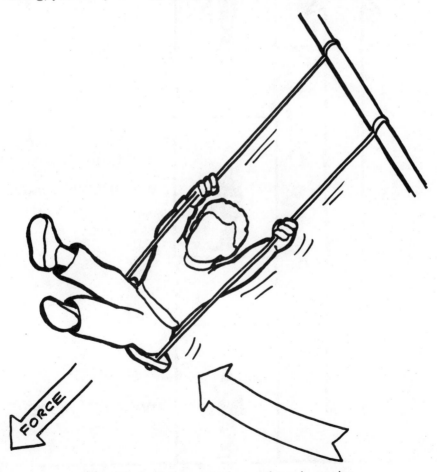

FORCE

Fig. 31-1. You can experience g-forces in a swing.

ity and your momentum as you stop going down and start going back up.

You can measure these forces by standing on the scales in an elevator. Watch the scales record your weight as the elevator starts to accelerate upward (Fig. 31-2). Notice your weight as the elevator

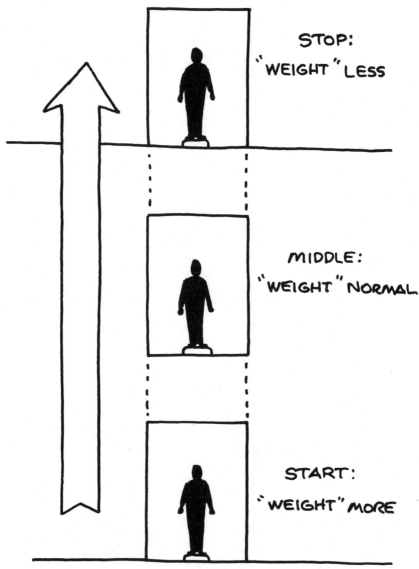

Fig. 31-2. *Read the scales as the elevator goes up.*

moves steadily. Now watch the numbers when the elevator comes to a stop. Repeat the experiment as the elevator descends (Fig. 31-3).

You really weigh the same all the time. It is the force that makes you feel heavier. Your body pushes back against this force with an equal force. When the elevator starts down, it doesn't push as hard against you, so your body doesn't push back as hard. This causes the scale to read less.

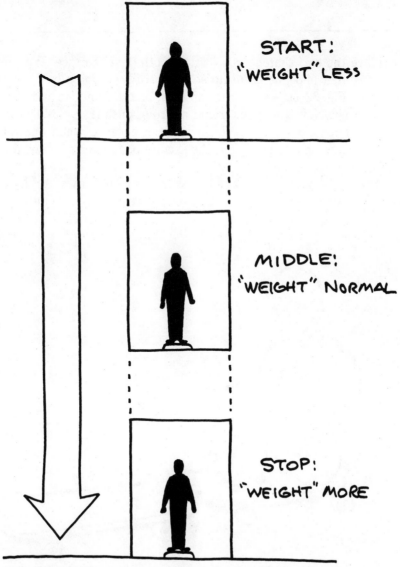

Fig. 31-3. *Notice how your weight changes as the elevator comes down.*

Experiment 32

Materials

- ☐ 2 skateboards
- ☐ 2 people of about the same weight
- ☐ smooth floor

Equal but Opposite Forces

Place the two skateboards on a smooth, level surface. Put them close together and line them up so they are both going in the same direction (Fig. 32-1). Ask your friend to sit on the front one and you sit on the other. Now give your friend a strong push (Fig. 32-2). Notice that you both moved apart. This happens because when one body exerts a force on another body, the second body exerts an equal but opposite force on the first body.

Try the experiment again but with a much heavier or lighter friend. Notice that this time the heavier person tended to move less

Fig. 32-1. *Place the skateboards on a smooth surface.*

Fig. 32-2. *When both people weigh about the same, both move apart equally.*

(Fig. 32-3). Try it again, only this time, push against a wall. You will move away from the wall because the wall is attached to the earth. This means you are pushing against the mass of the earth (Fig. 32-4).

Fig. 32-3. *If one person is smaller, the heavier person moves less.*

Fig. 32-4. *Pushing against a solid wall is the same as pushing against the mass of the earth.*

Experiment 33

Centripetal Force and Satellites in Orbit

Materials

- ☐ rubber stopper from a sink or bathtub
- ☐ the barrel, or tube, from an old ball point pen
- ☐ string (about 6 feet long)
- ☐ several flat metal washers
- ☐ 2 large paper clips

Tie one end of the string to the stopper (Fig. 33-1) and thread the other end of the string through the barrel. Run the string through the small, or pointed, end of the barrel toward the larger opening as shown in Fig. 33-2. Now run the end of the string through a few of the wash-

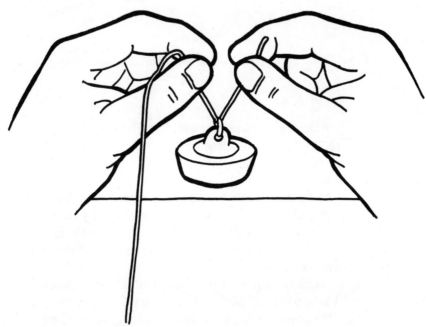

Fig. 33-1 *Tie the string to the stopper.*

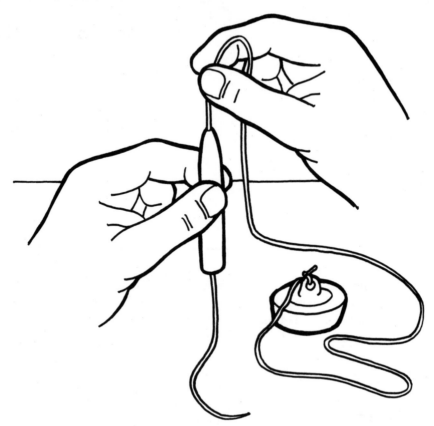

Fig. 33-2. *Thread the string through the barrel of the pen.*

ers. Tie a loop in the end of the string and attach one of the paper clips to the loop (Fig. 33-3). This will keep the washers from falling.

Hold the barrel in your hand and swing the stopper around in a circle. Start with a circle with about a three-foot radius. This will allow the washers to be suspended about three feet below the barrel. Add or subtract washers until the orbiting stopper is balanced by the washers. This will represent a satellite in orbit. The satellite is held in its orbit by the weight of the washers (Fig. 33-4). The weight of the washers supplies the centripetal force.

In space, gravity supplies the centripetal force to keep small bodies in orbit around larger bodies. Centrifugal force created by the movement of the satellite tries to make it leave its orbit. Centripetal force tries to keep the satellite in orbit (Fig. 33-5).

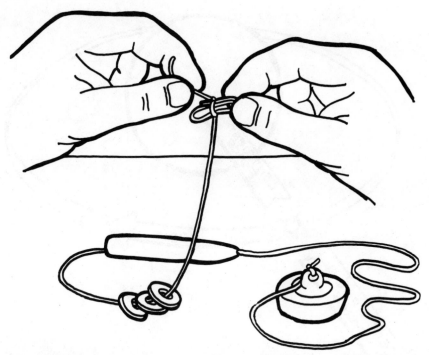

Fig. 33-3. *Slip the washers on the string and attach the paper clip to the end.*

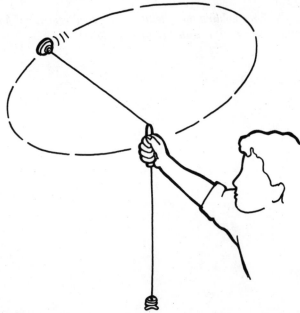

Fig. 33-4. *The weight of the washers should keep the stopper in a stable orbit.*

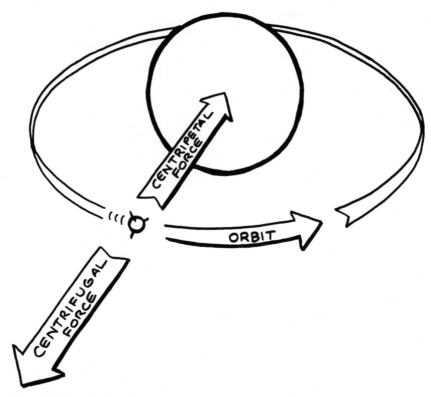

Fig. 33-5. *The force holding the satellite in is called centripetal force and the force pulling the satellite out is called centrifugal force.*

Experiment 34

Gravity and Mass

Materials

- ☐ soft ball
- ☐ golf ball
- ☐ 2 sheets of paper the same size
- ☐ high platform (upstairs window or porch)

Make sure the area is clear below you. Then hold the balls side by side and release them at the same time (Fig. 34-1). Both balls will strike the ground at the same time even though the golf ball is lighter (Fig. 34-2). The heavier soft ball has more mass than the lighter golf ball. The force of gravity pulls on all bodies the same, regardless of shape, size or weight.

Now crumple one of the sheets of paper into a ball and drop both pieces at the same time (Fig. 34-3). The ball of paper will fall much faster, even though they both weigh the same. This happens because of the resistance of the air (Fig. 34-4). A feather and a cannon ball will fall at the same speed in a vacuum.

Fig. 34-1. *Hold the balls at the same height.*

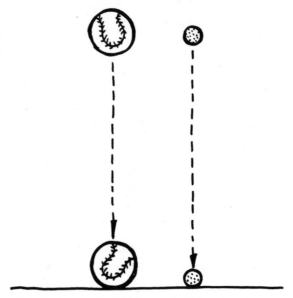

Fig. 34-2. *Both balls should hit the ground at the same time.*

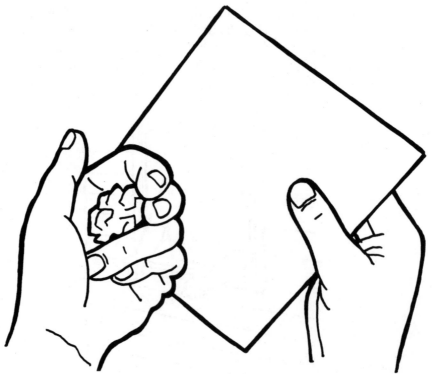

Fig. 34-3. *Crumple one of the papers into a ball.*

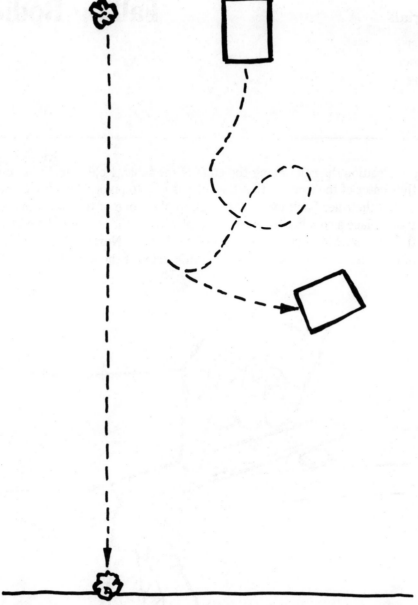

Fig. 34-4. *The resistance of the air affects the speed of the falling bodies.*

Experiment 35

Gravity and Falling Bodies

Materials

☐ ruler
☐ 2 coins
☐ table

Position the ruler along the edge of the table. Hold your finger on the center of the ruler so that the ruler is free to pivot. Now move one end of the ruler back just far enough to place one of the coins on the table. Place a coin in this space. Now place the other coin on the end of the ruler sticking out over the edge of the table. Next strike the edge of the ruler so that it will knock the first coin off the table (Fig. 35-1).

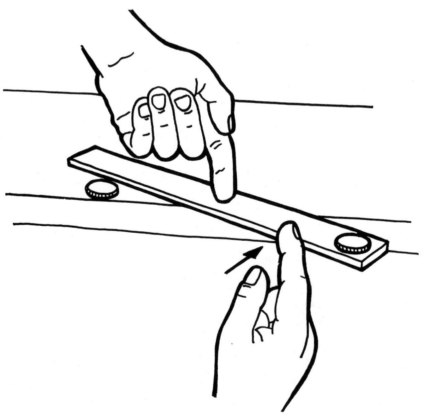

Fig. 35-1. *Strike the edge of the ruler.*

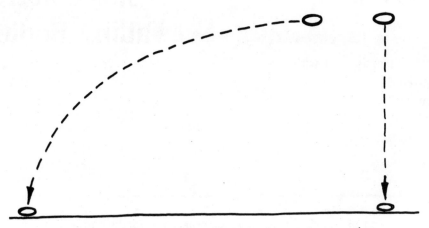

Fig. 35-2. *Both coins should hit the floor at the same time.*

The second coin should drop straight down. Listen for the sound of the coins hitting the floor. Try to determine if they both hit the floor at the same time (Fig. 35-2). They should.

If a ball is thrown perfectly level with the ground, and at the same time, another ball is dropped from the same height, the thrown ball will travel farther but they both will hit the ground at the same time (Fig. 35-3). The horizontal motion does not change the rate of fall of the bodies.

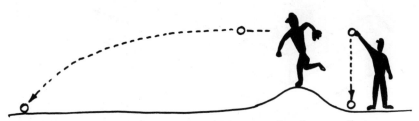

Fig. 35-3. *Both balls should hit the ground at the same time.*

Experiment 36

Materials

- ☐ flexible plastic ruler with a groove
- ☐ marble
- ☐ table
- ☐ tape measure

Speed and Falling Bodies

Stand one end of the ruler near the edge of the table. Bend it to form a curved ramp or slide (Fig. 36-1). Now place the marble about

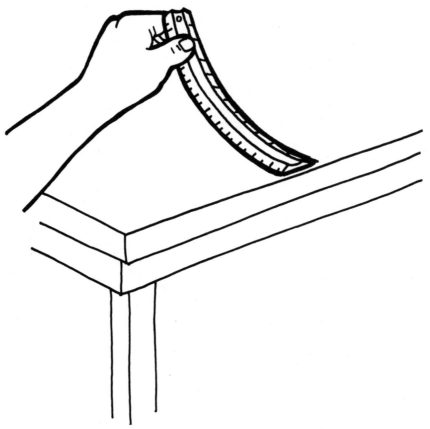

Fig. 36-1. *Use a flexible ruler for a ramp.*

half way up the ramp and release it. Measure how far it goes before it hits the floor (Fig. 36-2). Now try it again, only release the marble from three-fourths of the way up the ruler. Measure this distance (Fig. 36-3). Repeat the experiment once more but release the marble from the top of the ramp. Measure this distance.

Each time, the marble should have gone a little farther. When the marble was released from each higher point on the ramp, its speed increased and it left the ramp at a higher speed (Fig. 36-4). This caused the marble to travel farther each time.

If an object was launched from a very high point and its speed was increased until its rate of fall matched the curvature of the earth, the object would orbit the earth. This would require a speed of about 18,000 miles an hour (Fig. 36-5).

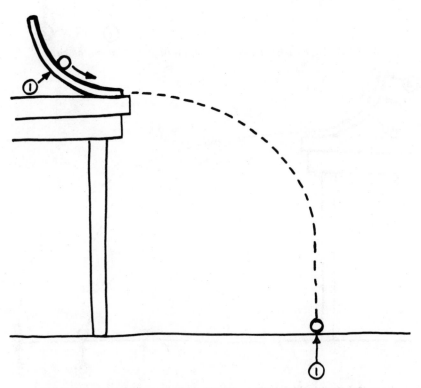

Fig. 36-2. Measure to the point where the marble hits the floor.

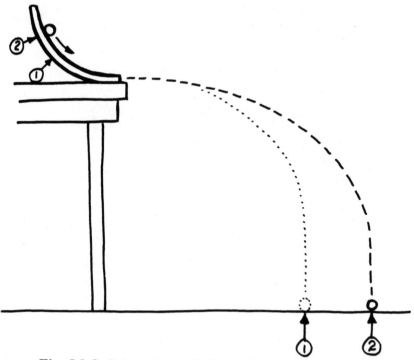

Fig. 36-3. Release the marble from a higher point on the ruler.

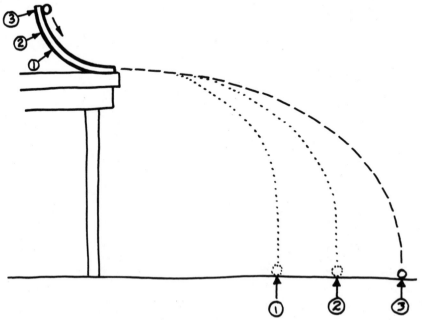

Fig. 36-4. *The higher the point of release, the farther the marble goes.*

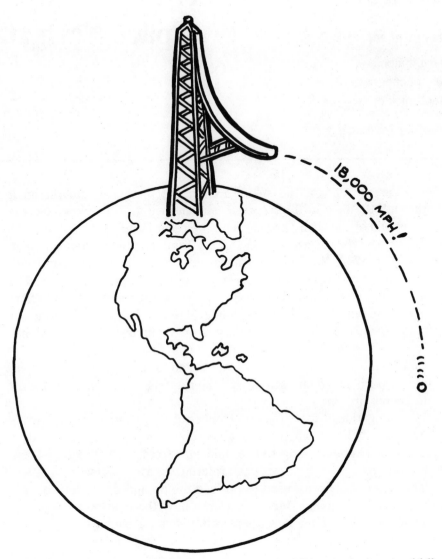

Fig. 36-5. *If the marble was released from a point high enough, its rate of fall could match the curvature of the earth.*

Experiment 37

Materials

- ☐ string (about 4 feet long)
- ☐ old phonograph record
- ☐ toothpick or small stick

The Gyroscope and Space Navigation

Tie one end of the string around the toothpick and thread it through the hole in the record as shown in Fig. 37-1. Now hold the other end of the string and suspend the record a few inches above the floor. Start the record to swing slowly from side to side like a pendulum (Fig. 37-2). Notice how it tilts around as it swings back and forth.

Now try it again but before starting it to swing, hold the record level and give it a spin (Fig. 37-3). This time, the record seems to float above the floor keeping its position level (Fig. 37-4). It will continue to stay level until the record almost stops spinning. The record has become a gyroscope. As long as it is spinning, it will remain in the same plane or attitude it had when it began to spin. This is why a spinning top will stand on its point and the rotating wheels of a bicycle try to keep it upright.

Navigation in space is a problem because it is outside of the earth's magnetic field. Magnetic compasses don't work. Stars are used as check points but it takes time to take star fixes. The gyroscope accurately provides the directional references for precise navigation. Three gyroscopes are used to provide the up and down, left to right and back to front axis. Most space craft have three or more navigation systems so that if one fails, there will be two for backup.

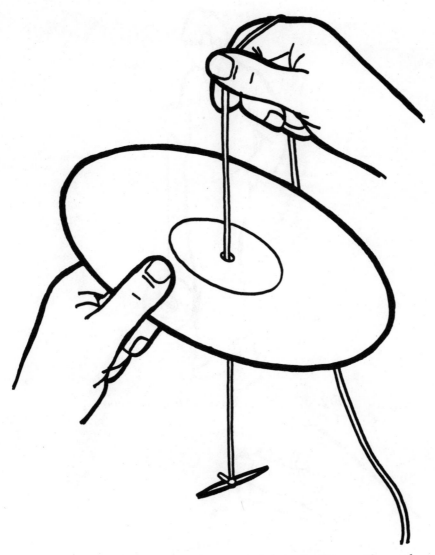

Fig. 37-1. *Thread the string through the hole in the phonograph record.*

Fig. 37-2. *Swing the record like a pendulum.*

Fig. 37-3. *Start the record spinning.*

Fig. 37-4. *The record will maintain a level attitude.*

Experiment 38

Energy in Space

Materials

- ☐ candle
- ☐ matches
- ☐ 2 shiny tin cans the same size
- ☐ 2 thermometers
- ☐ water (cold and warm)
- ☐ pliers

Using the flame from the candle, blacken the outside of one of the cans (Fig. 38-1). The other should be shiny. Put a thermometer in each can and fill each can about two-thirds full of cold water (Fig. 38-2). Set the cans side by side in warm sunlight. Monitor the changes in the temperature. The water in the dark can will begin to warm first (Fig. 38-3). The radiant heat from the sun strikes both cans equally, but the shiny can reflects most of the heat while the dark can absorbs most of the heat.

Now empty the cans and fill them about two-thirds full of warm water (Fig. 38-4). This time, place them side by side in the shade and again watch the change in the temperature. The water in the dark can will start to cool first (Fig. 38-5). The warm water causes both cans to radiate heat, but in the shade, heat will radiate faster from the dark surface. In space, sunlight can be easily converted into heat energy.

Fig. 38-1. *Blacken the outside of one of the cans.*

Fig. 38-2. *Fill each can with cold water.*

Fig. 38-3. *The water in the blackened can will start to warm first.*

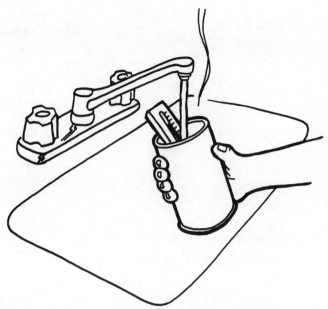

Fig. 38-4. *Fill each can with warm water.*

Fig. 38-5. *Place the cans in the shade. The water in the dark can will start to cool first.*

Experiment 39

Growing Plants in Space

Materials

- ☐ 2 cups the same size
- ☐ 1 tall jar
- ☐ 1 glass
- ☐ 2 identical strips of paper towel
- ☐ water
- ☐ food coloring
- ☐ table
- ☐ scotch tape

Place the two cups on a level surface (a table or counter top). Place the jar behind one of the cups (Fig. 39-1). Lower one end of one of the strips into the cup that is in front of the jar. Have the end of the strip just touching the bottom of the cup. Tape the other end to the top of the jar. Next lower one end of the other strip into the same cup like the first strip. Stretch this strip level with the table and tape its end to the edge of the other cup (Fig. 39-2). You'll have both strips in the same cup with one running straight up and the other bending to lay horizontal.

Now fill the glass with water and add a little food coloring (Fig. 39-3). This will make the water easier to see. Fill the cup with the two strips in it with the colored water (Fig. 39-4). Fill it to the top. Watch the colored water move along the two strips. The water is filling the tiny spaces between the fibers that make up the paper towel. Water is cohesive. This means it holds together. When water begins to fill the spaces, it pulls more water with it. This is called capillary action.

There are similar tiny spaces in the stems of plants. This is how plants feed. Notice how the water moves along the strip laying horizontal. After a few minutes you can see that the water travels faster along the strip laying flat (Fig. 39-5). This means that gravity slows the movement of the water traveling along the strip running straight up. Plants might grow faster in the weightlessness of space because the effects of gravity would not be present.

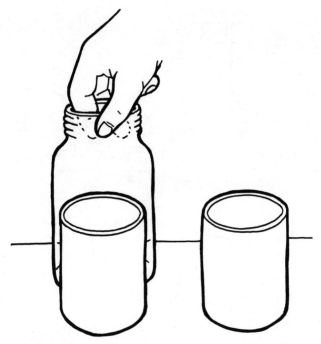

Fig. 39-1. *Place the jar behind one of the cups.*

Fig. 39-2. *Place the strips into the cup and tape the other ends in place.*

Fig. 39-3. *Add a little food coloring to the water.*

Fig. 39-4. *Fill the cup with both strips with the colored water.*

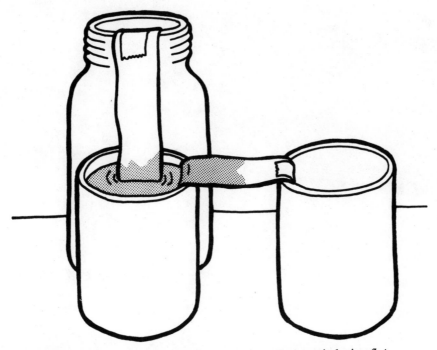

Fig. 39-5. *The water moves faster through the strip laying flat.*

PART II

Science Fair Projects

Science Fair Projects

Science fair projects are exciting but they do require a lot of planning (Fig. 40-1). Probably the most important part of the planning is deciding on the subject. Give this a lot of thought. Often when a subject is chosen too quickly, it is discovered later that the materials were not available, or were too expensive, or that the subject was just too complicated. When this happens, the project is usually abandoned and it might be too late to start another. Pick a subject you like. It should be one you are familiar with or would like to learn about. Put your imagination to work, but keep your project within your abilities.

Fig. 40-1. A science fair project requires planning.

Start by dividing your science fair project into basic steps such as: (1) Choosing a topic (2) Forming questions and hypothesis (the hypothesis is simply your guess of the results of the experiment) (3) Doing the experiment and (4) Recording results and forming conclusions.

You probably will need to make a report on your experiment. The report should show what you wanted to prove or the question you wanted to answer. Graphs and charts can be very helpful in explaining projects. Your report should describe the experiment, the results, and the conclusions you made.

When deciding on a project, choose a topic that you're really interested in. You should be enthused about your project. A simple experiment, well demonstrated, can be much more successful than a complicated one that is not performed very well. Often, major scientific breakthroughs are discovered using simple equipment.

Once you have chosen a subject, you'll want to display your experiment. It might be necessary for you to build a model. Usually these can be made from wood or cardboard. Don't overlook items that are normally thrown away. This could include empty coffee cans, plastic or glass bottles, cardboard tubes from paper towels or tissue, and empty wooden spools from sewing thread. Be creative. Use your imagination.

After you have selected the topic of your project, choose a specific question to be answered. Don't generalize. Have a definite problem to solve or a point to prove. For example; if you wanted to show how the light from a star can provide information about the star, you could build a spectroscope and examine the light from a candle or small lamp (Fig. 40-2).

You might build the tin can planetarium and project the northern polar constellations (Fig. 40-3). If it was made so that it could turn, you could prove that the North Star is located almost directly over the earth's North Pole. A time lapse photograph of the North Star will demonstrate how the constellations rotate around the North Star.

A shiny tin can, with one side painted flat black, could be mounted near a lamp to demonstrate how heat can be generated in a space craft. The tin can could be made into a model of a satellite or space craft. It could be mounted so that it could rotate on its axis. A thermometer could be used to measure the temperature as the space craft rolls the dark side toward the sun (Fig. 40-4).

Fig. 40-2. *A spectroscope can be used to examine light.*

You might want to display your experiment on a table. You could place it in front of cardboard or wooden panels. The panels could be in three sections. The two end panels can be angled forward so that it will stand by itself, like the back part of a theater stage.

The panel can show the information from your report (Fig. 40-5). The left side of the panel could show the purpose of your experiment, why you chose that project or what you wanted to prove. The middle of the panel could show how your experiment was con-

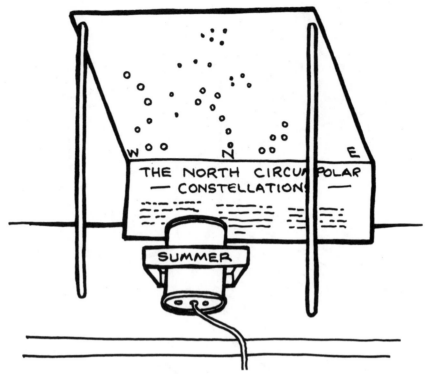

Fig. 40-3. *A tin can planetarium can be used in several ways.*

Fig. 40-4. *A project could show how heat energy can be generated in space.*

Fig. 40-5. Information about your project can be mounted on a panel.

structed. The right side of the panel could show the results of your experiment. It could include conclusions you've made and possible uses for this information (Fig. 40-6).

By using your imagination, you can expand and develop a simple experiment into a very interesting and enlightening project. Most any experiment has been done before, but your approach might be a little different. Use a different point of view. Change it around a little. Ancient man began studying the stars and wondering about space. A lot has been learned since then, but there are certainly many new discoveries yet to be made.

Fig. 40-6. *The information on the panels can tell the story of your project.*

Glossary

altitude—The angular height of a planet, star, etc. above the horizon.

astrolabe—An instrument formerly used to find the altitude of a star, etc.; it was replaced by the sextant.

azimuth—The angle along the horizon relative to north.

capillary action—The movement caused by surface tension and other forces of a liquid through tiny openings in a solid.

centrifugal force—The force tending to pull a thing outward when it is rotating rapidly around a center.

centripetal force—The force tending to pull a thing inward when it is rotating rapidly around a center.

Earth's magnetic field—The magnetic force surrounding the Earth from the magnetic north pole to the magnetic south pole.

g-force—Gravitational force; a force of attraction between any two objects because of their masses.

gyroscope—A small heavy wheel rotated at high speed on anti-friction bearings.

hypothesis—A guess used by scientists to explain how or why something happens.

International Date Line—An imaginary line drawn north and south through the Pacific Ocean, largely along the 180th meridian, where each calendar day begins at midnight.

lines of latitude—Lines drawn around the Earth, parallel to the equator, on maps and globes. They are used to indicate distances and locate points on the Earth's surface in relation to the equator.

lines of longitude—Lines drawn from north to south on maps and globes to indicate distances and locate points.

lunar eclipse—When the moon is hidden by the shadow of the Earth.

nadir—The point of the celestial sphere directly opposite to the zenith and directly below the observer.

Northern Hemisphere—All areas of the Earth's surface lying north of the equator.

planet—Any heavenly body that shines by reflected sunlight and revolves about the sun.

prime meridian—The meridian from which longitude is measured both east and west. Zero-degree longitude. It passes through Greenwich, England.

radiate heat—To send out heat in rays.

refracted—A bent ray of light.

solar eclipse—When the moon moves between the Earth and the Sun, so that we cannot see the sun.

Southern Hemisphere—All areas of the Earth's surface south of the equator.

spectroscope—An optical instrument used for studying the band of colors formed when a beam of light is separated into its different wave lengths.

star—A heavenly body, like our sun, that is self-luminous.

theodolite—An instrument used to measure vertical and horizontal angles.

vacuum—A space empty of matter.

zenith—A point in the sky directly overhead. A point directly opposite the nadir.

Index

INDEX

Other Bestsellers of Related Interest

COMPUTERS: 49 Science Fair Projects
—Robert L. Bonnet and G. Daniel Keen

This collection of step-by-step science fair projects—using PCs and BASIC programming—challenges students ages 8 through 13 to think logically and apply the principles of scientific inquiry. Students will explore biology, physics, math, and meteorology as they develop games of chance, aircraft design tests, mathematical conversions, and much more! 190 pages, 75 illustrations. Book No. 3524, $16.95 hardcover, $9.95 paperback

EARTH SCIENCE : 49 Science Fair Projects
—Robert L. Bonnet and G. Daniel Keen

This is an excellent resource for cultivating a better understanding of planet Earth among children ages 8-13. By studying the forces at work around them, they develop an appreciation for the foundations of science—concise thinking, clear notes and data gathering, curiosity and patience—which can carry over to every aspect of their lives. Projects include: growing crystals, solar distillery, erosion, weather forecasting, and more. 160 pages, 43 illustrations. Book No. 3287, $16.95 hardcover, $9.95 paperback

PHYSICS FOR KIDS: 49 Easy Experiments with Mechanics—Robert W. Wood

What makes a barometer work? Why can a flat rock skip across the water? Find the answers to these and many more physics puzzles here. Forty-nine fun experiments challenge students to think about the forces at work around them. Quick, safe, and inexpensive, the projects in this book produce results in less than 30 minutes (making them great for science class!) and require only common household items to complete. 160 pages, 165 illustrations. Book No. 3282, $16.95 hardcover, $9.95 paperback

PHYSICS FOR KIDS: 49 Easy Experiments with Optics—Robert W. Wood

Young readers ages 8-13 will enjoy these quick and easy experiments that provide a thorough introduction to what light is, how it behaves, and how it can be put to work. Wood provides projects including: making a kaleidoscope and a periscope, an ice lens, and a pinhole camera; and learning why stars twinkle, and how a mirror works. Projects produce results often in less than 30 minutes and require only common household items to complete. 178 pages, 164 illustrations. Book No. 3402, $16.95 hardcover, $9.95 paperback

PHYSICS FOR KIDS: 49 Easy Experiments in Electricity and Magnetism—Robert W. Wood

What makes a magnet stick to the refrigerator? What makes the batteries in a flashlight work? Find the answers to these questions, and more, in this entertaining and instructional project book. These quick, safe, and inexpensive experiments include making items like: a magnet, potato battery, flashlight, compass, telegraph, model railroad signal, and electric lock. 142 pages, 151 illustrations. Book No. 3412, $16.95 hardcover, $9.95 paperback

PHYSICS FOR KIDS: 49 Easy Experiments with Heat—Robert W. Wood

This volume introduces thermodynamics, or the physics of heat, to students ages 8-13. By performing these safe, simple experiments, kids can begin to understand the principles of conduction, convection, and radiation. Experiments show students how to: make a thermometer, make invisible ink, measure body heat, pull a wire through an ice cube, all quick, safe, and inexpensive, with results in less than 30 minutes. 160 pages, 162 illustrations. Book No. 3292, $16.95 hardcover, $9.95 paperback

"I MADE IT MYSELF": 40 Kids' Crafts Projects—Alan and Gill Bridgewater

This easy project book will give children hours of fun crafting toys and gifts with inexpensive household materials. Children will enjoy making musical instruments, kites, dolls, cards, masks, papier-mache and painted ornaments, as well as working toys such as a wind racer, land yacht, or moon buggy. Along with easy-to-follow instructions, each project includes scale drawings, step-by-step illustrations, and a picture of the finished item. 224 pages, 165 illustrations. Book No. 3339, $19.95 hardcover, $11.95 paperback

SCIENCE FOR YOU: 112 Illustrated Experiments—Bob Brown

"Has the advantage of including many different activities for younger students."

—School Library Journal

Every one of these challenging, entertaining experiments require only inexpensive and readily available materials. Step-by-step instructions, detailed explanations, and exceptionally well drawn with: electricity and magnetism, liquids, gases, sound and vibrations, seeds and plants, chemistry and physics. 128 pages, 112 illustrations. Book No. 3025, $12.95 hardcover, $7.95 paperback

Look for These and Other TAB Books at Your Local Bookstore

To Order Call Toll Free 1-800-822-8158
(in PA, AK, and Canada call 717-794-2191)

or write to TAB BOOKS, Blue Ridge Summit, PA 17294-0840.

Title	Product No.	Quantity	Price

☐ Check or money order made payable to TAB BOOKS

Charge my ☐ VISA   ☐ MasterCard   ☐ American Express

Acct. No. _____ Exp. _____

Signature: _____

Name: _____

Address: _____

City: _____

State: _____ Zip: _____

Subtotal $ _____

Postage and Handling
($3.00 in U.S., $5.00 outside U.S.) $ _____

Add applicable state and local
sales tax $ _____

TOTAL $ _____

TAB BOOKS catalog free with purchase; otherwise send $1.00 in check or money order and receive $1.00 credit on your next purchase.

Orders outside U.S. must pay with international money order in U.S. dollars.

TAB Guarantee: If for any reason you are not satisfied with the book(s) you order, simply return it (them) within 15 days and receive a full refund.   **BC**